Jewish Holidays
All Year Round

Marc Chagall, *The Story of Exodus: Moses Receives the Ten Commandments*, 1966.

Jewish Holidays All Year Round

A Family Treasury

Written by Ilene Cooper

Illustrations by Elivia Savadier

Captions by Josh Feinberg

In association with The Jewish Museum, New York

ABRAMS BOOKS FOR YOUNG READERS, NEW YORK

For the Palmer Rothman family:
Nancy, Steve, Ben, and Lily, with love

Thanks to Karen Sulak for her hamantashan and haroset recipes.
Special thanks to a skilled editor, Laaren Brown

—I.C.

For Stanley and Sadye, in the spirit of Eitz Chayim
—E.S.

Designer: Carole Goodman
Manager of Curatorial Publications, The Jewish Museum: Michael Sittenfeld

This publication has been made possible by a generous grant from the Keller–Shantoff Foundation.

Elivia Savadier's drawings for this book were created with pen and ink.
This book is set in 12-point Cochin.

Library of Congress Cataloging-in-Publication Data
Cooper, Ilene.
Jewish holidays all year round: a family treasury / written by Ilene Cooper ;
illustrated by Elivia Savadier in association with The Jewish Museum, New York.
p. cm.
ISBN 0-8109-0550-7
1. Fasts and feasts—Judaism—Juvenile literature. 2. Jewish crafts—Juvenile literature.
3. Cookery, Jewish—Juvenile literature. I. Savadier, Elivia. II. Jewish Museum (New York, N.Y.). III. Title.
BM690.C65   2002
286.4'3—dc21   20001056741

Printed and bound in China
10 9 8 7 6 5

HNA ■■■■■
harry n. abrams, inc.
a subsidiary of La Martinière Groupe
115 West 18th Street
New York, NY 10011
www.hnabooks.com

Contents

foreword

Welcome. Open this book and you open a door to The Jewish Museum, where we have hundreds of objects that people have used throughout the ages to celebrate Jewish holidays. In this museum art and artifacts are kept safe so that people can learn about the past and how Jewish holidays began many, many years ago. Some holidays relate to the time the Jewish people lived in the Middle East and their lives were bound up in the seasons, for the seasons determined when crops were to be planted and harvested. Other holidays relate to the stories of the Bible—to the life of Moses, or the heroic efforts of Queen Esther, or the courage of the Maccabees, as Jews won their freedom from enemies. We use objects, such as a matzoh cover on Passover, or a shofar on the Jewish New Year, or a noisemaker on Purim, to do very particular things on each holiday—to make a sound, to beautify a ceremonial meal, or to touch, feel, and hear the meaning of the holiday. The purpose of a museum is to save these objects so that you and your children and grandchildren can visit and learn about the long history of the Jewish people. Welcome to The Jewish Museum, and happy holidays!

Joan Rosenbaum
Helen Goldsmith Menschel Director
The Jewish Museum, New York

Laugh. Sing. Create. Dance. Celebrate. Reflect. Enjoy a wonderful journey through the Jewish year with your family, friends, and community. We hope this book will serve as a guide for you to find new ways to bring the spirit of the Jewish year into your homes.

Carole Zawatsky
Director of Education
The Jewish Museum, New York

Preface: The Jewish Calendar

The story of the Jewish people goes back thousands of years. Judaism, the religion that we follow, is blend of laws, prayers, history, legends—and holidays. On these special days throughout the year, we are asked to recall our history, to renew ourselves, to celebrate the earth's bounty, and to remember what it means to be Jews.

This book, beautifully illustrated by art and artifacts from the collection of The Jewish Museum in New York, introduces the Jewish holidays to young people. It explains the history and meaning of each holiday and shows readers how the holiday is observed both in the synagogue and at home. In addition, there are activities, crafts, and recipes to help personalize the holiday for families.

Different Jews—Orthodox, Conservative, Reform, Reconstructionist—may observe the Jewish holidays in different ways. In *Jewish Holidays All Year Round,* I have chosen to emphasize the similarities and the unity of our people.

The Jewish calendar is one way in which we are all united. As you read this book, you will notice that the Jewish calendar is different from the calendar commonly used in the United States and elsewhere in the Western world. The calendar we are so familiar with is based on the movement of the earth around the sun and has 12 months and 365 days in a year plus 4 hours, 48 minutes, and 46 seconds. This extra time is added up, and once every four years, a day is added to the month of February. We call the year in which February has 29 days a leap year.

The Jewish calendar is a lunar calendar; *lunar* is another word for moon. The Jewish people calculate their calendar according to the movement of the moon. It takes the moon approximately 29 1/2 days to move around the

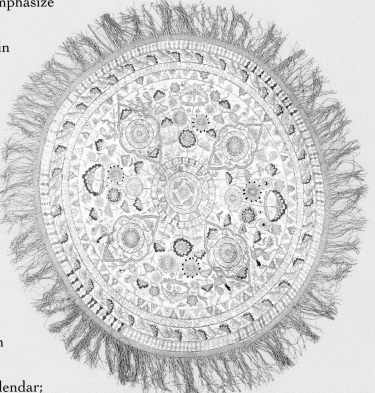

Sabbath Cloth, Persia, 1806. Sabbath and holidays are made more special by the objects we use to celebrate them. This elaborate cloth from Persia helped make the Sabbath unique and different from all the other days of the week.

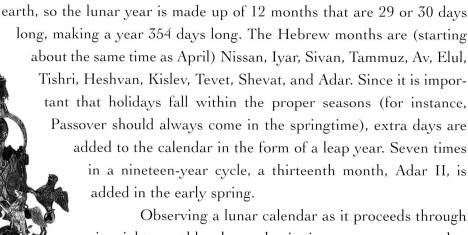

Torah Crown, Galicia, 1764/65, 1773. This Torah decoration blends Jewish symbols with the the signs of the zodiac. Can you see Gemini ("the twins") and Taurus ("the bull") in this picture? The Jewish artists borrowed the zodiac signs from the Greeks as a way to mark the months of the year.

earth, so the lunar year is made up of 12 months that are 29 or 30 days long, making a year 354 days long. The Hebrew months are (starting about the same time as April) Nissan, Iyar, Sivan, Tammuz, Av, Elul, Tishri, Heshvan, Kislev, Tevet, Shevat, and Adar. Since it is important that holidays fall within the proper seasons (for instance, Passover should always come in the springtime), extra days are added to the calendar in the form of a leap year. Seven times in a nineteen-year cycle, a thirteenth month, Adar II, is added in the early spring.

Observing a lunar calendar as it proceeds through its eight monthly phases, beginning as a new moon that builds to a full moon and then wanes to a thin crescent, binds Jews around the world to the rhythms of the moon.

In the fourth century C.E., a rabbi named Hillel II devised rules regarding the Jewish calendar. Before then, people relied on their wise men and leaders to inform them each month on Rosh Hodesh when their holidays would occur.

Rosh Hodesh, the monthly "holiday" for the new moon, comes from a Hebrew phrase meaning "head of the month." In biblical times, the high court of Jerusalem would announce the start of a new moon based on actual observation. Then people would count forward to determine the dates they needed to celebrate that month's holidays. But news traveled slowly in the ancient world. People could not be sure they were count-ing from the exact date of the new moon. And so to allow time for everyone to receive the information about the new moon, holidays lasted for two days. In the Hebrew calendar, each day begins at sunset and ends with the next sunset.

The Jewish calendar is one of the oldest calendars in use in the world. It begins with the traditional date of the Creation, 3761 B.C.E.; in other words 3,761 years before the beginning of the Western calendar. This book is being published, according to the Jewish calendar, in the year 5762.

So many of our stories are told in the Jewish holidays. The more we know and understand the Jewish holidays, the more we appreciate the beauty of Judaism, which has withstood tyranny and brought the sacred into everyday life for thousands of years. These holidays, which continue in an unending cycle, remind us all of the strength that is Judaism.

The Sabbath

Most holidays are celebrated just once a year, but the Sabbath is a holiday that comes every week. The Sabbath is a holiday in the truest sense: it is a special day that gives us an oasis of family togetherness, and peace after the week of school or work. This is the day to appreciate your mother and father, your sisters and brothers, your aunts and uncles, grandparents, cousins and friends and neighbors. It is the perfect time to gather them around you and rejoice in health and happiness.

The Sabbath is the oldest of the Jewish holidays, and the only one mentioned in the Ten Commandments. (It is number

Isidor Kaufmann, *Friday Evening*, c. 1920. Peace and serenity surround this young woman as she prepares for the Sabbath. Unfortunately, the artist, Isidor Kaufmann, never finished his painting. How would you complete the picture?

four: "Remember the Sabbath and keep it holy.") The Torah tells us that God created the world in six days, and on the seventh day, rested. According to the Jewish calendar, the last day of the week is Saturday, so the Sabbath, or *Shabbat* in Hebrew, begins at sundown on Friday evening and continues until sundown on Saturday. Like God, we rest on the seventh day.

Until the Ten Commandments brought the idea of the Sabbath, there was no such thing as a day of rest. Farmers, shepherds, those who worked (and that was almost everybody!) labored every day. It never occurred to anyone to do otherwise. Now, people worldwide have embraced the idea of a day of peace and rest. The Sabbath is a Jewish idea that has changed civilization.

The Torah tells us that on the Sabbath no work shall be done — so we can really celebrate. The Sabbath says: step back from your busy life, forget about homework and piano lessons and cleaning your room for a little while. The Sabbath is a moment in time and space to find peace, to go back to the harmony and tranquillity that Adam and Eve first found in the Garden of Eden.

Preparation for the Sabbath begins before sundown on Friday, when the holiday starts. The house is cleaned and the food is prepared; the braided loaves of bread, the *challah,* are put on the table, covered with a special cloth. Candles and wine are set out. There is a tradition that the Sabbath is like a bride or a queen; this image invites us to think of the Sabbath as an honored guest who is welcomed into the home with happiness and song.

The Sabbath begins as two candles are lit. We say a prayer. "Praised are You, O Lord our God, Ruler of the Universe, Who has sanctified us and commanded us to kindle the Sabbath lights."

After the candles are lit, a prayer, called the *kiddush*, is said over the wine cup. It begins, "Praised are You, O Lord our God, Ruler of the Universe, Creator of the fruit of the vine."

The two loaves of bread receive their own blessing: "Praised are You, O Lord our God, Ruler of the Universe, Who brings forth bread from the earth." Tradition tells us that when the Israelites were wandering in the desert after Moses had led them out of Egypt, God provided manna, a sweet substance, for food. Before the Sabbath, he provided a double portion of manna, which is symbolized by the two loaves of challah. Some people hold the two loaves of bread together and lift them up during the blessing.

When the blessings are completed, it is time for a delicious dinner, often punctuated by songs.

In synagogue on each Sabbath, a portion of the Torah is read. The Torah, comprised of the first five books of the Bible, is written on a scroll of parchment; every synagogue has at least one Torah scroll. A section from the part of the Bible called Prophets, the *haftarah*, is also read.

Ludwig Y. Wolpert, *Havdalah Set: Plate, Kiddush Cup, Spice Container, Candlestick*, Jerusalem, 1950–55. The candle, wine, and sweet-smelling spices of the Saturday night havdalah ceremony give us a way to remember the Sabbath after it is gone. How do you hold on to special memories in your life?

By Saturday evening, after a day of rest and relaxation, it is time to say good-bye to the Sabbath. When three stars can be seen in the sky, the *havdalah*, a ceremony of separation, begins. A special braided candle is lit; wine is sipped; and we breath in the fragrance of spices, bringing the sweetness of the Sabbath into the week . . . the Sabbath, our day to dream, to hope, to imagine a more perfect world.

Sabbath Activities

The Sabbath dinner is a time for families to be together and usher in the day of peace and rest. One tasty item often on the Sabbath table is chicken soup. Make this simple recipe with the help of an adult. It takes some time, but everyone at the table will enjoy its steaming, golden goodness.

Chicken Noodle Soup

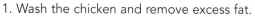

Ingredients:

1 large chicken, cut into quarters

10 cups water

1 tablespoon salt

1 medium yellow onion, peeled and cut into quarters

2 ribs celery with green top, sliced

2 carrots, sliced

1 sprig parsley

1/4 teaspoon pepper

1 chicken bouillon cube

8 ounces fine egg noodles

1. Wash the chicken and remove excess fat.

2. Put chicken in a large soup pot with water and salt. Use high heat to bring water to a boil, then cover. This takes about 20 minutes.

3. While the water is coming to a boil, prepare the vegetables. Turn down heat, so water is boiling gently. As the water boils, skim the excess fat, which looks like foam, with a large spoon. When all the foam is removed, reduce heat to very low. Add onion, celery, carrots, parsley, and pepper.

4. Simmer the soup, uncovered, for 1¹/₂ hours.

5. Remove boiled chicken. (It can be used to make chicken salad.)

6. Add the bouillon cube and stir. Cover the soup pot, and simmer for another hour.

7. Strain the soup into a saucepan. Now the saucepan holds only the broth from the soup.

8. Prepare noodles separately according to package directions. After noodles are cooked and drained, add to broth in saucepan, along with carrots and celery from the big soup pot.

9. Serve hot. This recipe makes eight servings.

Sand Candleholders

Materials:
sand of different colors, enough to fill two jars
  (available at craft stores)
2 small applesauce jars, washed with labels removed
2 white candles
metal tray

Note: You may work with both jars simultaneously or prepare them separately.

1. Pour sand of one color into a jar.

2. Tilt jar so sand makes a "hill" on one side of the jar.

3. Add sand of another color, making hill on other side and keeping colors separate.

4. Continue adding layers of sand in different colors.

5. Fill jar nearly to the top, then push in a candle so it stands erect.

6. Put candleholders on a metal tray before lighting the candles.

Rosh Hashanah

Everyone likes new beginnings. Rosh Hashanah is our chance to have a new beginning—and it comes every single year. We celebrate the beginning of the New Year on the first and second days of Tishri, which falls in September or October. This is the time to celebrate the beautiful circles and cycles that are so much a part of our Judaism now, as they have been for the past five thousand years.

The Jewish New Year is called Rosh Hashanah, which means "head of the year." The year is unmarked; a fresh start is possible. Everyone has a chance to begin anew. Rosh Hashanah is also the beginning of the High Holy Days, an important time on the Jewish calendar that culminates on Yom Kippur. During these ten days, Jews around the world think about how they have acted during the past year. They repent the things they have done wrong, and plan ways to do better in the future. That is why Rosh Hashanah ushers in a new beginning. It offers a chance to be kinder to your family and friends.

How can Rosh Hashanah be the beginning of the year when it comes during the seventh month of the Jewish calendar? Perhaps the most important reason for the Jewish year beginning at Rosh Hashanah is the legend that the creation of the world began on the first day of Tishri.

Also, in ancient times, Jews had several dates that marked the beginning of important seasons of the year. The first day of Tishri was the time when the old harvest year

Happy Jack, *Jewish New Year's Greeting*, Nome, Alaska, 1910. Happy New Year! Rosh Hashanah cards come in many shapes and sizes. Whether the card is printed on paper or carved on a walrus tusk, the sentiment is always the same—we wish our friends and families a sweet and happy year. An Inuit craftsman named Happy Jack carved the design on this "card" for a Jewish family in Nome, Alaska, in the early 1900s.

ended and the new harvest year began. It came during autumn, the start of the rainy season, a time that farmers and shepherds in ancient Israel anxiously awaited because rain meant a successful planting season.

There are other legends that have grown up around Rosh Hashanah. It is said to be the birthday of our patriarchs Abraham, Isaac, and Jacob, and the day when Joseph was freed from prison in Egypt. Abraham was ready to sacrifice his son Isaac to God on Rosh Hashanah, but Isaac was saved when God stayed Abraham's hand. In his place a ram was sacrificed (and perhaps that is one reason that the *shofar*, often made from a ram's horn, is so much a part of Rosh Hashanah celebration).

Rosh Hashanah begins, as all Jewish holidays do, at sundown. Families and friends gather together at the dinner table. As on every major Jewish holiday and the Sabbath, before the meal begins, a blessing is said over the candles. Then the prayer of thanksgiving for all things new, the *Sh'hehyanu*, is recited. Next comes the kiddush, the prayer over the wine, and the *hamotzi*, the blessing over the challah.

So far, this night seems like any Sabbath. But on Rosh Hashanah eve, the table differs in two ways from the Sabbath table. On the Sabbath, the holiday bread, the challah, is usually a braided oval loaf. On Rosh Hashanah, the bread is round, like a crown, reminding people that the holiday is the head of the year. The round loaf also reminds us of the unending cycles of life. Sometimes a little ladder or a bird perches on top of the loaf, symbolizing the wish that our prayers will go up to heaven.

Also on the table is a cut-up apple that is ready to be dipped in honey and eaten. The challah is quickly sliced for its honey dip, too. Everyone wants the first food that touches his or her lips on Rosh Hashanah to be sweet, ensuring a good and sweet year.

Rosh Hashanah services at the synagogue are a very important part of the holiday. It is a time when the congregation comes together to experience rebirth and renewal. A special prayer book called a *mahzor* is used during the High Holy Days. It is filled with prayers, songs, and stories that encourage people to think about what mistakes they have made during the last year and how they can redirect their lives. During the service a prayer called the *Unetaneh Tokef* proclaims that this is a time of judgment and tells people to choose repentance, prayer, and charity. Doing these things helps people to live a good life and promotes *teshuvah,* a return to God. Good thoughts and good works also remind us that there is always an opportunity to change and improve and get a new start in life.

An important part of Rosh Hashanah services is the blowing of the shofar. A shofar is an instrument made of a horn from a ram or another animal. Though the shofar can vary in length, it is often about a foot long and sometimes marked with designs. The shofar itself is hollow; the breath of the blower is what produces its sharp, intense sound. It is said that the shofar's upward curve allows its sound to go toward heaven; on earth, its sound awakens us. It asks us to pause and to reflect on this moment in time, and to ask ourselves what we will be like next year at this time. Will we be proud of how we have treated others and honored God?

Gabriel Cohen, *The Creation of the World,* 1980. According to the Bible, God created the world in seven days. Can you tell from this painting on which day God created the birds and fish? The moon and the stars? The animals? If you were going to create the world, what would you make first?

The shofar has played an important part in many moments of Jewish history. It is the same kind of horn Moses used to call his people to hear the Ten Commandments when he came down from Mount Sinai. It is also the horn that Joshua blew at the battle of Jericho. The Bible tells how the walls of the city shook with the noise until the walls came tumbling down, allowing Joshua and his army to enter and take the city. In modern times, the shofar was blown at the Western Wall when the Israeli Army liberated the Old City, and all of Jerusalem was reunited.

Legend says that on Rosh Hashanah the piercing sound of the ram's horn carries all the way to the ears of God, a reminder that it is time to open the Book of Life. The names of those who will live for another year will be inscribed in the book, and then the book will be sealed until next Rosh Hashanah.

During the Rosh Hashanah services, the shofar blasts a total of one hundred times. There are three distinct sounds: *shevarim,* three broken notes that sound like crying; *teruah,* nine intense notes that sound like wailing, and *tekiah*, one long, unbroken call. The job of blowing the shofar belongs to a member of the congregation called the Baal Tekiah. Blowing the shofar in the correct sequences is a difficult job—lots of breath control, not much time for thinking!—so sometimes the Baal Tekiah is guided by a reader who calls out the correct notes.

During the afternoon of the first day of Rosh Hashanah, many Jews observe the custom of *tashlich*, gathering at a body of running water, a river, lake, or stream. Adults and children throw their sins into the water symbolically, using breadcrumbs. The water washes the crumbs away, and with it our mistakes, large and small. Casting our sins away is one way to start the year fresh. Tashlich is also a nice chance for a nature walk with friends.

At the end of the service, the members of the congregation greet each other with the words *L'Shana Tovah*— "May you have a good year." According to Jewish tradition, after God opens the Book of Life on Rosh Hashanah, the fate of every Jew is decided. When people say L'Shana Tovah as a New Year's greeting, they are saying they hope that you will be inscribed in the Book of Life for a good year.

The Jewish New Year, although joyous, is not like the New Year's Day we celebrate on January 1 with parties and other noisy festivities. But one thing both celebrations have in common is that they mark a time to make resolutions about the ways we can change our lives for the better.

The Jewish New Year begins a time to look deep within ourselves. The ten days between Rosh Hashanah and Yom Kippur are sometimes called the Days of Awe, because we can feel God watching us as we think about the choices we have made in the past. We can also hear the small, quiet voice that lives inside each of us, reminding us of what we have done right and what we have done wrong.

These solemn days also give us great opportunity, if we take the time and effort to really think about the kind of people we'd like to be. How can we be better friends, better family members, better people? The answers to these questions can be found during the Days of Awe.

Chester Higgins, Jr., *Commandment Keepers Congregation Harlem (High Holidays)*, 1989. A shofar can be long or short, straight or twisted. Every shape produces a slightly different sound.

Rosh Hashanah Activities

New Year's Cards

It's time to wish friends and family L'Shana Tovah—Happy New Year! One special way to do this is by sending them holiday greeting cards. The custom of sending Jewish new year's cards began in Germany around the fifteenth century. The cards are usually decorated with symbols of the holiday: birds of peace, stars of David, shofars, the Book of Life.

Materials:
construction paper
crayons, paints, and/or markers
scissors
glitter glue

1. Fold a piece of construction paper in half.

2. Using crayons, paints, markers, glitter glue, or a combination, decorate the front of the card with a Rosh Hashanah symbol—either one listed above, or perhaps bees, honey jars, or apples.

3. Inside, write a personal message or a general one. Don't forget to say Happy New Year!

New Year's Greeting Card—Family Meal, Germany or United States, early 1900s. This wonderful pop-up card shows a family sharing a special meal.

Apple Honey Servers

Eating apples or pieces of challah that have been dipped in honey starts the year sweetly. Here's a way to make the apples themselves into honey servers. Using different varieties of apples adds to the festiveness of the holiday table.

Materials:
apples of different colors and varieties
apple corer (use with adult help)
melon baller (use with adult help)
knife (use with adult help)
small clean kitchen brush
lemon juice
honey
saucer or small plate for each apple

1. With the help of an adult, and using the apple corer, remove the apple seeds and the tough parts of the core, leaving the bottom intact so that the honey will not leak out. Use the melon baller to help hollow out part of the inside of the apple.

2. Carefully slice off the top of the apple and discard or eat. Brush the exposed parts of the apple with lemon juice to prevent browning.

3. Pour honey into the cavity of the apple.

4. Place each apple on a small plate or saucer.

5. Cut up other apples and bits of challah to dip into the honey, and place on the plate.

Yom Kippur

Yom Kippur, the Day of Atonement, is the holiest day of the Jewish year. This is the day when we ask God to cleanse us of our sins. It is a day to fast and pray, to take responsibility for our actions, to ask forgiveness for ourselves, and to forgive others.

When we hear that Yom Kippur is a day to repent for our sins, it is important to remember that in Hebrew, the word *sin* means "missing the mark." And haven't we all missed the mark? We've been mean when we should have been nice. We've been selfish when we should have been generous. We've ignored our responsibilities when we should have been helpful. Yet despite our failings, each year we have an opportunity to redirect ourselves.

During the ten Days of Repentance, the time that begins with Rosh Hashanah and ends with Yom Kippur, we have the opportunity and the obligation to think about the divide between the ways we have behaved and the better behavior of which we know we are capable.

Although missing the mark is a part of life, there are ways to repair whatever damage has been done. The great Jewish sage Maimonides, who lived during the twelfth century, offered three steps to true repentance.

First, think about what you've done.

Second, promise yourself that you will not make the same mistakes again.

Third, seek forgiveness.

Many people use the ten days between Rosh Hashanah and Yom Kippur to go to family and friends and ask that they be forgiven for whatever hurt they've caused during the year. God can only forgive the sins you committed against God. It is up to those you have wronged to forgive you for any personal misdeeds you have committed.

Yom Kippur is a day of fasting, so before sunset we eat a holiday

Ben Shahn, *Today Is the Birthday of the World,* 1955. The Hebrew words on this drawing by the artist Ben Shahn proclaim the birthday of the world. We celebrate this birthday and all the High Holidays by blowing the shofar, and reflecting on the year that has passed. How do you celebrate your birthday?

meal that is meant to sustain us through many long hours. After this dinner, healthy Jewish adults consume no food or drink until sundown on the next day. (Children under thirteen and the sick and elderly do not have to fast, but sometimes children as young as nine begin skipping a meal or two.)

Why do we fast on Yom Kippur? This is a time to ignore everyday matters, like food, while we concentrate on prayer. Also, fasting reminds us of those who are hungry every day. Yom Kippur gives us another chance to appreciate everything we have that we may take for granted—food, health, home, a loving family.

Before families leave their homes for the synagogue, parents may say a blessing over their children or light special *yahrzeit* candles that burn as a memorial to loved ones who have died. Then it is time to attend the Kol Nidre service, which is the centerpiece of Yom Kippur eve.

As you walk into the synagogue for Kol Nidre services at dusk, the awe of Yom Kippur can be felt all around. On Yom Kippur, the sanctuary is full. Many people wear white on this day, to symbolize a spiritual return to innocence and purity.

The service is led by the rabbi, and the cantor also chants a portion. Flowers sometimes decorate the *bimah,* the raised platform where services are held. Like the congrega-

Belt Buckle for the High Holidays, Poland, 1863. New clothes traditionally make the high holidays a special time. This silver buckle probably adorned a new outfit made especially for the occasion.

tion, the ark itself wears white—special white curtains reserved for this day. Even the Torah scrolls are covered in white cloth.

As the Torah is removed from the ark, the cantor begins to chant the Kol Nidre.

The melody of the Kol Nidre (translated from the Hebrew as "all vows") is both beautiful and haunting. The words ask that all personal vows, including religious vows, made thoughtlessly or in haste be annulled. Today, in our country, Jews live freely and openly—but sadly, in other times and other places, this has not always been true. There have been many times in history when Jews have been forced to make vows to other religions. Some say that the purpose of the Kol Nidre is to forgive those who throughout history have been forced to renounce the Jewish faith.

Another important prayer of the evening service is a prayer of confession during which seemingly every possible sin that may have been committed during the past year is called out. Each line of the prayer begins: "For the sin that we have sinned before You." The congregation pleads for forgiveness from the sins of lying, dishonesty, disrespect, stubbornness, and many many more. The prayers are always expressed in terms of "we" rather than "I," because as a community, we share these sins.

During the next day's service, this confessional prayer is repeated several times. "For the sin that we have committed by lying, for the sin we have committed by dishonesty, for all of these, O God, forgive us and pardon us," part of the prayer asks. Sometimes people tap their hearts as they say the prayer, to show that their prayers come from the heart.

As the day proceeds, with its prayers and chanting, the congregation expresses ever more fervently the hope for forgiveness. Yet each person also begins to formulate the ways he or she will do better in the coming year. The year is like a fresh piece of paper upon which anything can be written. What will you write?

During the afternoon, the biblical story of Jonah is read. In the story, God asks Jonah to go to the city of Nineveh to warn the people to end their evil ways or be destroyed.

Jonah does not want to do God's bidding. He wants the people to be punished for their sins, and he realizes that God will spare them if they change their ways. Then Jonah—having warned the people—will look like a false prophet.

To escape God's task, Jonah runs away to sea. When a huge storm blows up that could destroy everyone on board, the sailors wonder if someone on the ship is responsible for this natural disaster. Jonah confesses that he is escaping God's bidding—and the sailors promptly throw him overboard. A huge fish swallows him, but miraculously, he survives inside its belly. For three days and nights, Jonah prays to God to save him, and he promises to do what God has asked of him.

After the whale expels Jonah, he keeps his promise to God. He goes to Nineveh to give the citizens God's warning. The frightened people pray to the Lord and promise to give up their evil ways. And God does save them.

Jonah is not pleased. He thinks the people of Nineveh deserve to pay for their sinning. He goes and sits outside the city. It is hot, and God makes a gourd grow next to him; its large leaves provide him with shade. But then at night God causes a worm to eat the plant, which takes away the shade. Now Jonah is angry with God.

"Jonah," the Lord says, "you have pity for a plant for which you have not labored. It grew up in one night and disappeared in one night. Yet you have no pity for the thousands of people of Nineveh, My creations, and you are angry with Me for forgiving them."

Jonah then understands, as do the listeners in the synagogue, the importance of repentance and how God's mercy extends to all who repent.

Now the Yom Kippur service is drawing to a close. The final service, Neilah, the Closing of the Gate, ends the holiday. It is our last chance to express the hope that we will be sealed in the Book of Life. The final prayer is Judaism's holiest, the Shema: "Hear O Israel, the Lord our God, the Lord is One." A long steady note is blown on the shofar. The Gates of Heaven are closed. The time has come to go home, to break the fast with friends and family, and to feel the freshness of a new year and new beginnings.

Yom Kippur Activities

Yom Kippur Journal

Reflecting on how you have acted over the year takes some time and some thinking. This season of the year is a good time to start a journal. In it, you can write your innermost thoughts.

Buy a diary, journal, or notebook, and each day write about your successes and your shortcomings. Describe how you plan to do better. Write about your relationships with your family, your friends, your teachers, and other important people in your life. Don't forget to write about the many things in your life for which you are thankful. Put down on paper how you intend to become a better Jew: uphold your religion, be a better steward to the planet earth, and be more charitable to those around you.

Keep the journal for a year. Then, next Rosh Hashanah, read it through and see how well you have done in meeting your goals.

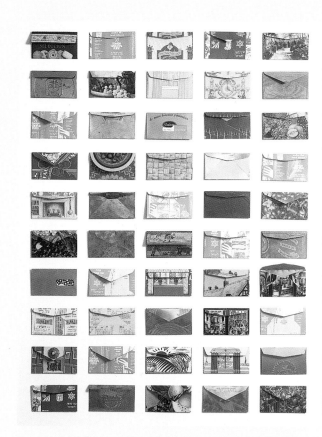

Harriete Estel Berman, *Tzedakah* (alms container), 1999. Yom Kippur is a time for serious thought and prayer. It is also an opportunity to help others by giving *tzedakah*, or charity. This unusual *tzedakah* box is made of fifty separate envelopes. If you could send each envelope to someone who needs it, who would you send them to?

Noodle Kugel

After sundown Yom Kippur ends, and it is time to break the fast with a light meal. Often one of the dishes included on the menu is *kugel,* a sweet noodle pudding. There are many recipes for kugel. This is a simple one to make with adult help.

Ingredients:
12–16 ounces medium noodles, cooked and
    drained according to package directions
4 ounces butter (one stick)
1 cup sugar
5 eggs
1/2 cup milk
3 apples, peeled and sliced
1 cup raisins
nonstick cooking spray
cinnamon

1. Preheat oven to 350 degrees.

2. Spray 9 x 13 inch glass or metal pan with nonstick cooking spray.

3. Melt butter in microwave.

4. Put cooked noodles in a large mixing bowl. Add melted butter to the cooked noodles.

5. Add remaining ingredients, mixing after each addition.

6. Pour ingredients into pan.

7. Sprinkle liberally with cinnamon.

8. Bake one hour, or until firm. Serve warm or cold.

Tzedakah Box

Tzedakah means justice. As you approach a new year, think about ways to make life better for those less fortunate than you. Many families have a tzedakah box in which they put money in honor of the Sabbath or holidays; when the box is full, the money is taken out and given to a favorite charity. Here is a simple way to make a tzedakah box of your own.

Materials:

coffee can or any large container with a plastic lid

colored paper or aluminum foil

colored pens or pencils

scissors

glue

1. Cut a piece of paper or foil long enough to fit around the can.

2. Decorate the paper or foil with symbols of the holiday or the words *charity* or *tzedakah*.

3. Wrap the paper or foil around the can and glue it on.

4. With adult help, cut or use a knife to make a slot in the lid.

5. Remember to put coins in the box before the Sabbath or holidays, or anytime you have some extra change.

6. Think of a charity you would like to help with your money. When your box is full, send the money off.

Alms container, Denmark, 1901. The Hebrew inscription on the side of this tzedakah box says, "Happy is he who considers the poor" (Psalms 41.2).

Sukkot

When the leaves begin changing color, and the High Holy Days have come to an end, it's time to celebrate Sukkot. This happy harvest holiday is celebrated in a special way—and in a very special place, a homemade hut called a *sukkah*.

What is the reason for the sukkah? The Torah says: "You shall live in huts seven days in order that future generations may know that I made the Israelites live in huts when I brought them out of Egypt" (Lev. 23:24).

This Torah portion refers to the Exodus from Egypt. The Israelites, who were led out of slavery by Moses, wandered through the desert for forty years before they reached the Promised Land. During that time they made huts, or booths, of wood and palm as their shelters. The Hebrew word for booths is *sukkot;* just one booth is a sukkah. The whole holiday is named after the booths.

The holiday Sukkot also recalls the time after the Israelites left Egypt and were finally settled in the Promised Land, a place called Canaan. There, many ancient Israelites were farmers. The autumn was the beginning of the rainy season, when the ground was moist for planting the winter crops of wheat and barley. It was also a time of harvest. Grapes were ready to be made into wine and olives into oil. But the crops had to be gathered as they ripened, or else they would rot.

Sometimes the land where the crops needed harvesting was too far away for the farmer and his workers to return home each night. So, like their newly freed ancestors who had made temporary homes in the desert, these Jewish farmers built sukkot and lived there until the harvest was finished.

Today, Sukkot is a week-long holiday that begins on the fifteenth of Tishri. The most essential part of the holiday is the sukkah. Synagogues build a communal sukkah, and many people build their own at home.

The walls of a sukkah can be made of any material—wood and cloth are common—and its roof should be made of something that once grew, such as tree branches or bamboo. A sukkah is always located outside. Only two walls and a part of a third need be constructed; one wall can be a fence or the side of a house. The roof must be open enough to let the stars shine through at night.

Once the sukkah is constructed, it is time to decorate it. Some people put carpets and fancy furniture inside; others use lawn furniture or a card table. The walls might be adorned with chains made of paper, popcorn, or berries. Fruit, vegetables, and flowers are also used as decorations; they add a festive note and remind people of the holiday's harvest origins.

Some Jews really do live in the sukkah during the seven days of the holiday. Most people, however, just eat meals there. Friends and family come to share these meals. Symbolic guests are invited, too: Abraham, Isaac, Jacob, Joseph, David, Moses and his brother Aaron, Sarah, Rachel, Rebecca, Leah, and Miriam are welcomed into the sukkah—biblical heros and heroines for every night of the holiday.

Four plants play their parts in the celebration of Sukkot. As the Torah says, "On the first day you shall take the fruit of goodly trees, branches of palm trees, boughs

Israel David Luzzato, *Sukkah Decoration*, Trieste, Italy, c. 1775. Using the ancient art of micrography—making designs out of tiny writing—this artist reproduced the entire text of the book of Koheleth (Ecclesiastes), which is read on Sukkot, on a paper only 15 1/2 inches wide and 20 inches tall.

of leafy trees, and willows of the brook, and you shall rejoice before the Lord." Each plant has its own special significance to the holiday.

The *lulav* is a branch of the palm tree. The *hadasim* are three boughs of a leafy myrtle. The *aravot* are two branches of a willow tree, and the *etrog* the lemonlike fruit of a citron. Branches from the three plants are bundled together. Together they are called the lulav, named for the largest part, the palm frond.

At home or in synagogue, each person can hold a lulav in his or her right hand with its spine facing the body. The etrog is held in the left hand with its stem down. The bless-

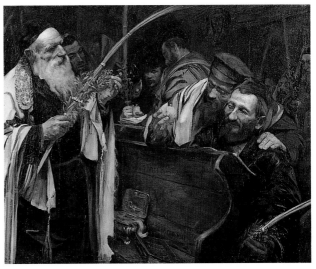

Leopold Pilichowski, *Sukkot*, 1894-95. An etrog must have a stem, or pitom, in order to be used on Sukkot. Take a close look at this painting. How do you think these men keep their etrogs safe when they are not using them?

ing, "Praised be You, O Lord our God, Ruler of the Universe, Who instructs us to shake the lulav," is recited, and the lulav is shaken once in each direction—north, south, east, and west, as well as up and down—to show that God is everywhere.

Traditions have sprung up around these four plants and why they are used. The lulav has no scent, but because it is the leaf of the palm tree that bears dates, it has a taste. The myrtle branches have no taste, but emit a wonderful smell. The willow has neither taste nor fragrance, but the etrog has both. The rabbis have compared the lulav to a person who has learning but ignores good deeds; the myrtle, to a person who has no learning but is kind to others; the willow, to a person who has neither learning nor does good deeds; and the etrog, to a person who has learning and is kind. Together these plants symbolize the variety of people who make up the Jewish community.

Sukkot is a holiday of rejoicing and thanksgiving. Does it remind you of Thanksgiving? It should. The Pilgrims, who came to America to escape religious persecution, were well versed in the Bible. Their trip from Europe was their Exodus and the New World was their Promised Land. In 1621, when they wanted to celebrate a good harvest, they looked to the Bible and to Sukkot for inspiration for their own Thanksgiving.

Today, each sukkah—fragile, cobbled together with wood and cloth, open to the sky and the rain—reminds us that we eternally owe our thanks to God. The sukkah symbolizes our need for God's shelter.

Sukkot Activities

Hanging Decorations

Although the sukkah is a temporary shelter, it is meant to look festive and pretty. Here are some ideas to get you started on decorating your sukkah. How many ways can you think of to use the holiday's harvest theme?

FLOWERS AND BRANCHES

Collect flowers, pretty weeds, or branches with leaves or berries. Tie them together with ribbon and hang them upside down throughout the sukkah. Hanging them upside down allows the sap to run into the flowers, and the color will be brighter.

PAPER AND POPCORN CHAINS

Cut colored construction paper into small strips. Dab a small amount of glue or paste on one end of a strip and fold into a circle, gluing one end to the other. Take the next strip and loop it inside the first circle and glue the ends together. Continue until you have a chain long enough to drape around the sukkah.

Pop a bowl of popcorn and string the kernels on a long thread or a thin wire. Cranberries may be used as well.

Louis Goldman, *Sukkot Market, Tel Aviv, September 1953.* Looking for the perfect lulav and etrog this year? Finding a good set takes a sharp eye, a keen nose, and just the right touch.

Model Sukkah

Make a miniature sukkah to keep in your room or inside the real sukkah. The base of the little sukkah is made from clay and the walls are wooden craft sticks. The roof is twigs.

Materials:
molding clay
wooden craft sticks
items to decorate the sukkah
twigs, some with leaves
disposable aluminum tray

Note: Make the sukkah on the tray for easy mobility.

1. Make three substantial clay strips about one inch tall, two of the same length, about six inches long, and one several inches longer. The longer piece is the base for the back wall of the sukkah. The two shorter pieces are for the side walls. Mold an end of a shorter strip to one end of the longer strip. Do the same with the other short strip.

2. Push the craft sticks vertically into the clay base at even intervals, leaving a small space between sticks. Press sticks in tightly.

3. Decorate the inside of the sukkah with dollhouse furniture or items you make yourself, such as tiny dried flowers or berry bouquets. Draw small pictures for the walls and hang with tacks. Cut rugs out of pieces of material.

4. Use the twigs to make the roof of the sukkah. Lay the twigs in the spaces between the craft sticks.

Etrog Ball

The etrog is a fragrant yellow citron. During the services the fruit lies nestled in a box with cotton to protect it. After Sukkot is over, you can save the etrog, because it will not rot. It will get smaller and blacker, but it will keep its delicate scent. To preserve the etrog, prick it all over with a toothpick. Then stick in cloves. Put the etrog ball in a drawer or closet and enjoy it all year round.

Simchat Torah

Very soon after Sukkot, we welcome Simchat Torah, one of the most joyful days on the Jewish calendar. On this day, we rejoice in one of God's greatest gifts to us: the Torah. The Torah is the center of Jewish spiritual life, and Simchat Torah is a big rowdy party that invites everyone to join in the celebrations.

A Hasidic proverb says that during the High Holy Days, you serve God with every bit of your body. On Rosh Hashanah, you use your brain to remember; on Yom Kippur, you give your heart. On Sukkot, you serve with your hands by building the sukkah. And on Simchat Torah, it is your feet that serve as you march around the synagogue, dancing, singing, and thanking God for the great gift of the Torah. The name of the holiday means, literally, "rejoicing in the Torah."

As it has for thousands of years, the Torah teaches Jews everywhere how to lead a good and worthy life. The Torah is made up of the first five books of the Bible: Genesis, Exodus, Leviticus, Numbers, and Deuteronomy. Genesis begins with the story of the creation of the world, and Deuteronomy ends with the death of Moses after he has led the children of Israel to the Promised Land.

A Torah scroll is the most precious and beloved object in any synagogue. Some synagogues have only one Torah scroll; others own several. The scroll is made of a special parchment that can only be written on by hand. A *sofer*, or scribe, is specially trained for this task. It takes the sofer a year to handwrite a Torah, and every letter and mark must be executed perfectly.

All year, during each Sabbath service, a portion of the Torah is read. On Simchat Torah, the year's worth of reading comes to an end—and starts all over again.

Simchat Torah began a thousand years ago, but our contemporary celebration started during the Middle Ages. The evening service at the synagogue is a noisy, joyous occasion. Before passages from the Torah are read, all of the Torah scrolls in the synagogue are taken out, and the *hakafot*—a merry parade—begins. The scrolls are carried aloft, circling the synagogue seven times. The congregation follows, dancing and singing, with the children right beside the grown-ups, waving colorful flags and, often, collecting candy that is showered upon them.

The morning service for Simchat Torah is equally joyous. Children under the age of thirteen have a special role in the service: They are called to recite the blessing over the Torah. Even the youngest boys and girls are able to participate in this honor.

The person who reads the last portion of the Torah is called the bridegroom of the Torah, because the happy mood of the day is like that of a wedding, and the bridegroom is perhaps the luckiest and happiest of all the people at the "wedding." As soon as the last portion is read, the book of Genesis is opened and the reading of the Torah begins anew. Just as the reading of the Torah never ends, neither does the study of Torah.

Why would you read a book more than once? The Torah is no ordinary book. Every time you read it, new meanings emerge. Now, while you are young, the lessons of the Torah may seem very straightforward, and the stories may seem like ordinary stories. But as you grow older and change, the way you read the Torah will change, too. Stories and ideas that may once have seemed simple become richer and more complex. Familiar pieces from the Bible such as the temptaion of Adam and Eve in the Garden of Eden and the rivalry of Cain and Abel are stories with many layers. Peel back one, and you will find another to examine. Sometimes the Torah is compared to an onion! To study Torah is to peel back layers of meaning and always find more to think about. Often in synagogue you will hear about the Tree of Life. (You will hear this much more than the "Onion of Life"!) When people say Tree of Life, they are talking about the Torah—a tree that is the main source of religious and moral nourishment for Jews around the world.

Simchat Torah Flag, Poland, 1800s. This flag was made by pressing ink onto paper with a carved wood block. Although it was made to celebrate Simchat Torah, the picture shows a different holiday.

Simchat Torah Activites

Simchat Torah Flag

Flags are an important part of celebrating Simchat Torah. Make a flag of your own so you can wave it during holiday services.

Materials:
several pieces of construction paper,
  9 by 12 inches, any color
piece of cardboard, 9 by 12 inches
glitter glue, various colors, and
  white glue
flat wooden stick from a craft store,
  approximately 12–15 inches long
stapler (use with adult help)

Torah Shield, Nuremberg, c. 1720.
A Torah shield adds to the beauty of
a Torah scroll and symbolically protects
it from harm. This shield uses flowers,
bells, and animals—both real and
imaginary—to honor the Torah.

1. Using a pencil, draw symbols of the holiday—a Torah scroll, an apple, a Star of David—on construction paper.

2. Using different colors of glitter glue, fill in the designs. Let dry.

3. Cut out the designs. Use the white glue to adhere the cut-outs to a fresh piece of construction paper.

4. Using the white glue, stick the new paper to the piece of cardboard.

5. Staple the cardboard to the stick.

Solomon Alexander Hart, *The Feast of the Rejoicing of the Law at the Synagogue in Leghorn, Italy,* 1850. Dressed in their finest and carrying the Torah scrolls for all to see, these men celebrate Simchat Torah. Can you find all ten scrolls in this painting?

Caramel Apples

Apples are one of the holiday's traditional symbols, and caramel apples are a favorite treat. You will need craft sticks to make the "handles."

Ingredients:
1 pound caramels, unwrapped
2 teaspoons water
4–6 small apples

1. Place caramels and water in a small pot. With the help of an adult, heat over a very low flame until caramels melt, stirring frequently.

2. While the caramels are melting, push a craft stick into each apple.

3. Dip apples in melted caramel and let cool on wax paper.

Hanukkah

Who can retell the things that befell us?
Who can count them?
In every age, a hero or sage
Came to our aid.

     — "Who Can Retell?"

The words of this traditional Hanukkah song introduce us to a favorite holiday on the Jewish calendar: Hanukkah, the eight-day Festival of Lights. The holiday celebrates religious freedom and honors a band of rebels who stood up for Judaism against a tyrant king and his large, well-equipped army.

The story begins in 175 B.C.E., when Antiochus IV became king of Syria, the country that ruled over Israel, then called Judea. The Jewish people, so often conquered by the more powerful, wanted only to be left alone to observe their own customs, celebrate their holidays, and have the freedom to worship the one God as they wished.

But Antiochus had a different idea. He insisted that

Larry Rivers, *Study for Maccabees II*, 1982. When Judah Maccabee and his brothers took back the holy Temple from the Syrians, they found statues of Greek gods where the altar should have been. According to artist Larry Rivers, what happened next?

the Jews turn their back on all that was holy to them and worship the Greek gods. Then, deciding that he, too, was a god, Antiochus ordered the people to worship him.

The Jews of Judea were angry and scared. Many of those who defiantly continued to practice Judaism were tortured and killed. Then, in the village of Modin in 168 B.C.E., soldiers came to force any remaining Jews into giving up their beliefs. An old man named Mattathias was so enraged at the heathen altar in his village that he killed a traitorous idol worshiper as well as some of the Syrian soldiers.

Fleeing to the mountains with his five sons, Mattathias organized a renegade band to fight the king and his army. The guerillas were led by Mattathias's son Judah, who was nicknamed "the hammer"—in Hebrew, HaMakkabi. Today we call Judah and his followers the Maccabees.

Although many came and joined the revolt, Antiochus did not take this ragtag army very seriously. He had weapons and trained soldiers. He even had thirty-two elephants decked out in armor. They carried baskets with sharp-shooting bowmen who were ready to rain arrows down on their opponents.

However, the Maccabees had one important thing the Syrian army didn't have: a fierce determination to liberate their country and reclaim the freedom to practice their religion.

For three years the Maccabees made night raids that weakened the Syrian army. Then they fought a ferocious battle in which they took back Jerusalem and drove the Syrians back to their own land. They had won!

But when at last the Maccabees reached the great temple in Jerusalem, a sickening sight met them. The Temple, the very heart of Judaism, had been grossly defiled by the king's army. Statues of Greek gods and goddesses were everywhere; the Torah scrolls had been torn to pieces. Pigs' blood had even been spilled on the holy altar. The great seven-branched *menorah*, meant to burn with an eternal light, stood dark and neglected.

The Maccabees scrubbed and cleaned the Temple and built a new altar. But when they went to light the menorah, there was no oil to be found. They searched everywhere, and finally, a small vial of the precious oil was discovered. It was hardly enough to last one day, and it would take time for new oil to arrive. Still, the Maccabees were happy to be able to light the lamp at all.

Then a great miracle occurred. The oil, which should have been gone by nightfall,

Mae Rockland Tupa, *Hanukkah Lamp, "Miss Liberty,"* Princeton, New Jersey, 1974. Hanukkah is a celebration of freedom—both in the time of the Maccabees and today. The artist who made this Hanukkah lamp used American symbols of freedom.

kept the menorah lights burning for eight days, until new holy oil could be brought.

This story holds great symbolism for the Jewish people. It speaks to the miracles that can happen when we stand up for what we believe is right. And it reminds us that what starts as a small flicker of hope can burn brightly in the hearts of women and men for a long, long time.

The rededication of the Temple that took place on the twenty-fifth of Kislev is celebrated today as the holiday of Hanukkah, a word in Hebrew that means rededication. It comes in December, sometimes in the early part of the month, sometimes closer to Christmas.

Hanukkah is a holiday of light, feasting, festivities, and fun. At the center of the Hanukkah celebration is the lighting of candles in a special candleholder called a menorah. The Hanukkah menorahs used today have nine branches, one holder for each of the eight nights of the holiday (because the oil burned for eight days), and one for the candle that is used to light the others. This candle is called the *shamash*, which means servant in Hebrew.

Each night of the holiday one candle is added to the menorah, so on the first night of Hanukkah, there is one candle plus the shamash in the menorah; on the second night there are two plus the shamash, and so on.

A menorah can be any shape or style, but all of the candleholders, except for the shamash, should be at the same height. Over the centuries there have been menorahs carved of wood and shaped from clay or metal. Sometimes they are adorned with religious symbols, and sometimes they are more abstract, even whimsical.

F. J. Kormis, *Hanukkah Lamp*, London, England, 1950. Flanked by mighty lions, Judah Maccabee prepares for battle. Lions, a symbol of strength, are the emblem of the ancient tribe of Judah.

This is how to light the Hanukkah candles: The candles to be lit on each night are placed in the menorah, starting at the right, and moving to the left. The shamash is the first to be lit, and it is used to light the other candles (that is why it is called the servant — it serves the other candles). The lighting is done from left to right, so the newest candle is the first one that is lit each night. Then the shamash is put in its holder.

There are two blessings that are said with the lighting of the candles. In English, the first is "Blessed are You, O Lord our God, Ruler of the Universe, who has sanctified us and commanded us to kindle the lights of Hanukkah." The second is "Blessed are You, O Lord our God, Ruler of the Universe, who performed miracles for our ancestors in those days, at this time." Often we sing traditional songs such as "Maoz Tzur" ("Rock of Ages") or "Who Can Retell?" after the blessings.

The candles are lit each night after sunset and should burn at least half an hour. Your family might use one menorah, or you may have one for everyone in the family — truly a festival of lights. Put your menorahs in a window so that the miracle of Hanukkah can be proclaimed to everyone. Some families like to guess which candle's flame will last the longest, with each child choosing a different candle. It is easy to get distracted by the festivities and miss the flames going out, but there is always the next night to watch more closely.

Once the candle lighting is finished, the festivities begin! Hanukkah is a holiday of delicious food and happily received gifts. It is a time to make memories with families, sharing games, songs, and laughter.

Many of the happy memories people have of Hanukkah start with the food, especially potato *latkes*. (Latkes is the Yiddish word for pancakes.) This treat is made by mixing grated potatoes and chopped onions together with eggs and flour. Then the latkes are usually fried in oil and eaten with sour cream or applesauce. Oil, an important part of Hanukkah lore, also plays an important part in

Hanukkah Lamp, North Africa, c. 1900. Six tiny birds are perched gently on this Hanukkah lamp. Can you find them all?

Hanukkah Lamp, Stolin, Russia, c. 1885. Each of these chairs is just two and a half inches tall—too small for sitting, but just the right size for a Hanukkah light. These little chairs brought joy and warmth to Russian Jews at Hanukkah time.

the food of the holiday. In Israel, oil is used to fry special doughnuts called *sufganiyyot*.

When the feasting is over, it is time for more singing and dancing and to play a game of chance called Dreidel. The *dreidel* is a spinning top with a Hebrew letter on each of its four sides. At Hanukkah, many families also exchange presents, small and large. If your gift is Hanukkah *gelt* (money in Yiddish), then you can use the pretty chocolate coins wrapped in gold or silver foil to play Dreidel. Sometimes the gelt is real coins. They are also good for playing Dreidel.

Hanukkah is a happy holiday that both adults and children look forward to all year long. Everyone likes to get gifts, but the greatest gift of all is the religious freedom that Hanukkah celebrates. Take this time to join your family in rejoicing.

Dreidels, Poland, 1700s. These dreidels were carved from wood more than two hundred years ago. Which one would you like to play Dreidel with?

Hanukkah Activities

Potato Latkes

Potato latkes are the food most associated with Hanukkah. This delicious treat isn't difficult to make, but because grating and cooking in hot oil are involved, adult help is required for the preparation. Be sure to eat all the crispy bits that fall off the edges of the latkes!

Ingredients:

5 medium potatoes

1 small onion

2 tablespoons flour

2 eggs

vegetable oil

nonstick cooking spray

1/4 teaspoon salt

1/4 teaspoon pepper

1. Peel the potatoes.

2. Using a food processor, grate the potatoes. (You may use a hand grater, but watch your knuckles. They are easy to scrape!)

3. Grate onion into same bowl.

4. Drain liquid from mixture. Squeeze the potato-onion mixture in large handfuls over the sink to remove more liquid.

5. Beat the eggs in a separate bowl, and then add to potato-onion mixture.

6. Add flour, salt, and pepper. Mix well.

7. Spray nonstick cooking spray on a heavy skillet. Then pour in enough vegetable oil to cover the bottom of the pan. Turn heat to medium high.

8. Drop large spoonsful of the potato mixture into the hot oil. After the pancakes start to sizzle, flatten them with a pancake turner. When the pancakes crisp and their

edges turn brown, flip and cook on the other side. Add more oil as needed.

9. Serve hot, with applesauce or sour cream. Leftover latkes may be warmed in the oven or microwave.

Oven-Baked Latkes

Here is a recipe for latkes you bake in the oven rather than fry on the stovetop. The latkes have a nice even shape and make a good side dish. You will still need an adult's help for this recipe, but it is much easier than frying the latkes. Double the recipe and use two muffin pans if you would like more latkes . . . and who doesn't?

Ingredients:
2 pounds boiling potatoes (with thin skin)
3 small onions, chopped fine
3 tablespoons cooking oil
2 eggs
1/2 teaspoon salt
applesauce and sour cream, for serving

1. Preheat the oven to 400 degrees.

2. Grate the potatoes coarsely and put them in a colander in the sink.

3. In a pan, sauté the onions in 2 tablespoons of oil, then set aside.

4. While the onions are cooling, squeeze the water from the grated potatoes.

5. When drained, put the potatoes in a large bowl and add the onions, eggs, and salt. Stir.

6. Oil a nonstick 12-muffin pan. Divide the potato mixture evenly among the muffin cups. Drizzle a little oil over the top of each unbaked latke.

7. Put the loaded muffin pan into the hot oven. Bake for about 45 minutes or until the latkes are firm and browned. Take the pan out of the oven and use a butter knife to loosen the latkes.

8. Serve hot, with applesauce and sour cream.

Dreidel

The traditional Hanukkah game of chance is called Dreidel. One of the best things about Dreidel is that it can be played by just two people, or many more. Age is no problem, either; even little kids can quickly learn the game. All you need is a dreidel and fifteen or so small objects such as beans, pennies, or small candies for the players to use for betting.

A dreidel is a small top with a Hebrew letter on each of its sides. The letters *nun, gimmel, hey,* and *shin* stand for the sentence "a great miracle happened there." There have been dreidels made of clay, lead, even expensive materials like silver and ivory. Most dreidels today are made of wood or plastic.

How to Play:

1. Each player puts one of his or her betting objects into the pot.

2. The first player spins the dreidel. The letter that comes up tells the player what to do. Nun (נ) stands for nothing; it is the next player's turn to spin. Gimmel (ג) means the spinner takes the pot. For hey (ה), only half the pile is taken. Shin (ש) instructs the spinner to put one piece into the pot.

3. The next player takes his or her turn.

4. Whenever the pot is empty, or there's only one piece left, every player has to put in a betting piece before the next spin.

The rules for Dreidel are loose, and there are many variations. One has players putting two betting pieces into the pot if shin comes up; another option says shin means putting in half your betting pile. The game can be over when one player loses his or her pot; whoever has the most is the winner. But some people play until one player has won everything and the rest of the players are wiped out.

Bonnie Srolovitz and Michael Berkowicz, *Executive Dreidel,* New York, 1993. Kids aren't the only ones who celebrate the miracles of Hanukkah. This dreidel puts a grown-up spin on the traditional Hanukkah toy.

Tu B'Shevat

Everyone loves trees. They provide fruit and nuts for food, and wood for making everything from paper to houses. Their shade keeps us cool in the summer; their logs keep us warm in the winter. For birds and squirrels and many other animals, the trees are homes. Tu B'Shevat, sometimes called the New Year of Trees or the Jewish Arbor Day, is celebrated on the fifteenth day of Shevat. This is the day to honor the trees, one of God's many gifts to all of us.

In the Bible, we are reminded of the value of trees; it tells us that even in the midst of war we are not allowed to destroy an enemy's trees (Deut. 20:19).

The Tree of Knowledge stood in the Garden of Eden. Noah built the ark of wood. King Solomon built the Temple in Jerusalem of cedar. The Psalms celebrate the willow and the

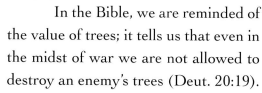

Anna Ticho, *Jerusalem Hills*, 1978. Israeli artist Anna Ticho creates an impression of the rugged, rolling hills outside Jerusalem with simple lines and subtle colors.

Samuel Halpert, *Trees*, 1917. Instead of people, the artist chose to make the trees the stars of his painting. If these trees could talk, what do you think they would say?

palm, and many, many fruits, including the fig and the citron, are mentioned throughout the Bible.

Tu B'Shevat is the time to celebrate trees in a very tangible way: by planting them. Although in most of North America the month of Shevat is too cold for planting, in Israel it is the beginning of spring. Because Israel is so dry and hot, the country needs trees to hold soil and prevent erosion—and of course to provide the many other boons that trees give us.

In 1900, the Jewish National Fund was established for the purpose of planting trees in the Holy Land, often with donations from Jews outside the country. Today, this holiday is a time when Israelis help restore their land by planting trees and vines.

Besides the planting of trees, there is no prescribed way to celebrate Tu B'Shevat. Many people like to eat fruit, especially those kinds that are found in Israel, such as figs, dates, and oranges, and nuts like almonds. Sometimes the fruit is eaten on special plates decorated with fruit. Many people also use the occasion to donate money or food to the poor, who may not be able to feed themselves.

In recent years, Tu B'Shevat has evolved beyond a celebration of trees. Now it is linked with protecting the environment and our responsibility to care for the earth. On Tu B'Shevat, we pause to think about what we can do to keep the land cleaner and healthier and to consider how we can help protect the environment.

However we observe Tu B'Shevat, by planting trees, or by working to help the environment in another way, we enter the spirit of this holiday. By honoring nature, Jews pay homage to those who came before them and show their love and respect for those who will come after them.

Tu B'Shevat Activities

Spring Cleanup

Although it may be too cold to do a cleanup of your yard when Tu B'Shevat comes around, plan on doing one in the spring. Rake leaves, pick up branches that have fallen during the winter, and place the yard waste in biodegradable bags. If your parents pay you for your cleanup, donate the money to a charity that has special meaning to you.

Annie Leibovitz, *Kibbutz Amir, Israel,* 1969. It's harvest time on Kibbutz Amir. Perhaps the workers have taken a short break from their labors. Maybe they are finished for the day.

Growing Plants

It's easy to grow plants inside no matter what the weather. Here are some simple ways to start a garden using common items found in the grocery store.

SWEET POTATO PLANT

Materials:

sweet potato (choose one with small, purple buds
  near the wide end)
jar or glass with a rim wide enough to hold the
potato
water
toothpicks
clay pot, 6 inches in diameter
potting soil

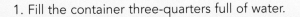

1. Fill the container three-quarters full of water.

2. Put the potato in the container with the bottom in the water and the buds at the top. Insert the toothpicks into the potato so that they touch the rim of the container and hold the potato upright.

3. Place the potato in a sunny spot. Water a little every day. Watch for leaves to sprout on top and roots below. This will take several weeks.

4. After a few more weeks you may plant the potato in a pot filled with potting soil. Keep soil moist as plant grows. In the late spring, put the plant in the garden outside.

PARSLEY FOR PASSOVER

Materials:

parsley seeds, flat-leaf or curly
planting tray with holes in the bottom for drainage
potting soil

1. Plant the parsley seeds in the planting tray according to package directions.

2. Place tray in a sunny window.

3. Water regularly so that soil is moist but not soggy.

4. A few sprigs of your parsley may be ready in time to use them on the *seder* plate at Passover.

Purim

A wise, beautiful heroine. The downfall of a murderous tyrant. The salvation of a community. Are these pieces of a fairy tale? No, but they are parts of the story of Purim, one of the happiest holidays on the Jewish calendar.

Purim, which is observed on the fourteenth of Adar (February or March), is an ancient holiday that goes back to the fifth century B.C.E. and commemorates the deliverance of the Persian Jews from certain destruction. Purim reminds us to be thankful for other times throughout our history when we were saved from persecution—and it reminds us to always keep Judaism in our hearts.

The story of Purim is in the part of the Bible called the Writings. Purim begins with Esther (Hadassah in Hebrew), a young Jewish woman who lived in Persia about 2,400 years ago. Esther, an orphan, was taken in by an older relative named Mordecai, who looked after her like a father. They lived in the royal town of Shushan, ruled by a gullible king named Ahasuerus.

One night, Ahasuerus was having a lavish banquet. Eager to show off his wife's beauty, he called for Vashti to present herself to his male guests. When Vashti boldly refused, Ahasuerus's advisors told him he must banish her and choose a new wife.

Many young women went to Ahasuerus's court, but the one he chose was the lovely Esther. Mordecai told Esther not to reveal that she was Jewish, so she kept this information to herself.

To stay close to Esther, Mordecai came each day to the gates of the palace. One day, as he sat in his usual spot, Mordecai heard two of the king's chamberlains plotting to kill Ahasuerus. Mordecai sent a message to Esther, who, in Mordecai's name, informed the king of the threat against him. Ahasuerus was pleased, and he had Mordecai's good deed written down in the palace records.

But someone else was not so pleased with Mordecai. The king's closest advisor was a wicked man named Haman. Haman was used to everyone bowing down to him when he passed. There was just one person who refused to bow to Haman, and that was Mordecai.

"I am a Jew," Mordecai explained. "I bow only to God."

That answer made Haman even more furious. He told the king, "There is a people scattered throughout your kingdom who do not keep the king's laws! If it pleases your majesty, let it be written that they be destroyed. I will even give ten thousand pieces of silver to the royal treasury to see this accomplished."

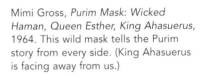

Mimi Gross, *Purim Mask: Wicked Haman, Queen Esther, King Ahasuerus,* 1964. This wild mask tells the Purim story from every side. (King Ahasuerus is facing away from us.)

The king did not really care who these people were, but he liked the idea of ten thousand pieces of silver coming into his treasury. He told Haman to do as he wished, on any day of Haman's choosing. Haman cast lots—a process that is something like rolling dice. It was determined that the massacre of the Jews, young and old, would begin on the fourteenth day of the twelfth month.

When he heard of the king's decree, a distraught Mordecai told Esther that she must go to Ahasuerus and save her people. Esther knew that no one was allowed to see the king without his invitation, on penalty of death. At great personal risk, Esther put on her best clothing and went to the king.

So lovely was Esther that when she appeared before the king he was not angry. He told her that she could ask of him anything, even half of his kingdom. But Esther, frightened, asked only that the king and Haman come to dinner in her private residence.

Haman was delighted with this honor. His happiness only increased when, at the private dinner, the king told Esther once more that anything she desired could be hers, and she requested that Ahasuerus and Haman come for dinner the next night.

Despite all the good things that were happening to him, Haman was still full of hatred for Mordecai. Haman's family encouraged him to erect a gallows on which to hang Mordecai. After all, he was planning to murder all the Jews; who would care if Mordecai met his end a bit sooner than the rest? Haman thought this was a very good idea, and he had the gallows built immediately.

That night, the king couldn't sleep, and he asked that the palace records be read to him. As he listened, he was reminded that Mordecai had once saved his life. "Has anything been done to reward this man?" Ahasuerus asked. When he learned that nothing had been done, the king called for Haman, and asked, "What should be done for a man the king wants to honor above all others?"

Robert Indiana, *Purim: The Four Faces of Esther*, 1967. Queen Esther is remembered on Purim for her courage. What do we remember about Mordecai, Haman, and Ahasuerus?

Haman was sure that the king was talking about him. "Such a noble man should be given the king's own robes, the king's crown, and paraded through the town on the king's horse," Haman suggested.

Ahasuerus agreed, and he told Haman to make sure all of this was done—for Mordecai.

A miserable Haman attended Esther's second banquet. This time, when the king asked her what wish she might like granted, Esther had an answer. "I ask for my life, and the life of my people."

Esther explained how Haman had deceived the king. Furious, Ahasuerus ordered Haman to be hanged on the gallows Haman himself had erected for the death of Mordecai. Then the king named Mordecai his new advisor. The fourteenth of Adar became a holiday to commemorate how evil was thwarted.

Today, Jews all over the world remember Esther's bravery and celebrate the salvation of the Jews of Persia. The name Purim comes from the Persian word *pur*, which means lots. Casting lots is like the throwing of dice, in which number come up by chance. It is how Haman chose the day of the Jews' destruction.

On Purim we are commanded to be happy! The holiday is celebrated in many ways, but always it begins with reading the story of Esther. Called the Megillah, or the Scroll of Esther, it is separate from the rest of the Torah, rolled on its own small scroll for easier handling, since the entire story is read from beginning to end at both the evening and the morning services.

Both readings are times for hilarity and fun. Adults and children come dressed in masks and costumes, and they bring noisemakers known as *groggers* with them. (Many temples pass them out to everyone before the reading, too.) Even the rabbi and the cantor may dress up in costumes! Some temples put on a funny show, singing parts of the story to the tune of new and familiar songs. As the Megillah is read, everyone listens for the name of Haman.

Each time, there are yells and boos, and the participants shake their groggers, making enough noise to drown out the hated name. Sometimes people write Haman's name on the bottom of their shoes, and they stamp their feet to wipe it away. The whole service is loud and raucous as everyone screams and yells and laughs at the show. This is a wonderful day to bring friends to services.

After the Purim service, the party continues with treats. One of the main items on the menu is *hamantashan*, a delicious pastry filled with a poppy seed, prune, or fruit mixture. The triangle-shaped cookies are said to look like the three-cornered hat that Haman wore. In Israel, these cookies are called *oznay Haman*, which means Haman's ears.

Sometimes, the Purim party becomes a carnival, with games and prizes for the best

Esther Scroll, possibly Moravia, 1700s. A scroll of Esther may include not only words, but also pictures that illustrate the story.

costumes. In Israel, an impressive carnival is held in Tel Aviv. Elaborate floats wind through the streets, as costumed revelers sing and dance.

There are other traditions associated with Purim. This festive occasion is a time to share with friends and family. Sending portions of food and wine is called *mishloach manot* in Hebrew, and you can even buy special paper plates decorated with scenes from the Megillah. This is also a time for tzedakah, when the poor are remembered with gifts of food or money.

Before Esther first approached King Ahasuerus, she told Mordecai to ask the Jews of Shushan to fast and pray along with her for the success of her mission. Now, in remembrance of Esther, many Jews fast the day before the holiday begins.

Another holiday tradition is that of the special Purims. The rabbis decreed that anyone—an individual or a community—who has experienced a miraculous deliverance from danger can make that day a Purim.

Not everyone agrees that the story of Purim is based on historical fact. But there is much to be learned from the Megillah about Jewish identity and our responsibility to the community. What all listeners take away from Purim is a sense of how an individual's bravery can stop a tyrant. During times when the Jewish people have been threatened, they have taken heart remembering the tale of Esther.

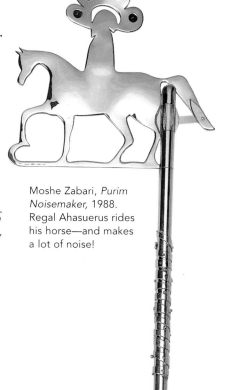

Moshe Zabari, *Purim Noisemaker*, 1988. Regal Ahasuerus rides his horse—and makes a lot of noise!

Purim Activities

Hamantashan

Here's a recipe for hamantashan that parents and children will enjoy making together.

Ingredients:
1/2 pound butter (two sticks), melted
8 teaspoons of sugar
3 1/4 cups of flour
2 teaspoons baking powder
1/4 teaspoon salt
2 eggs
3 teaspoons orange juice
2 teaspoons vanilla

Filling:
2 cups apricot butter or spoon fruit, or poppy seed
  or prune filling, or chocolate chips
1/2 cup ground almonds (optional)
2 teaspoons orange zest (optional)

1. Cream the butter and sugar.

2. Sift the dry ingredients together and add to the
   butter-sugar mixture. Mix well.

3. Add eggs, orange juice, and vanilla. Knead until
   dough forms a ball, then chill.

4. Divide dough into five sections. Roll out each section
   on a floured board.

5. Using a drinking glass as a cookie cutter, cut out circles.

6. Place a teaspoon of filling into each circle. Add a little ground almond or orange
   zest if you like. Form a triangle by pinching edges together.

7. Bake at 325 degrees for 25 minutes. Cool cookies on racks.

8. Serve hamantashan warm or cold.

Grogger

This sample noisemaker is perfect for the Megillah reading. Try different items inside the can. What makes the loudest noise?

Materials:

empty coffee can or any other container
   with a fitted plastic lid

scissors

construction paper

crayons

tape

handful of dried beans or pennies

1. Cut paper to fit around the container.

2. Decorate paper with drawings of Jewish stars or characters from the Purim story.

3. Tape decorated paper around the container.

4. Place beans or pennies inside the container and replace the fitted lid.

5. Shake the grogger and yell when you hear Haman's name!

Purim Noisemaker, Russia, 1800s. This noisemaker helps tell the story of Purim— as well as providing plenty of noise during the reading of the Megillah.

Passover

"Let my people go!" demanded one of Judaism's greatest leaders. These words, spoken by Moses to the Egyptian pharaoh, echo down through the ages. Moses was instructed by God to lead the children of Israel out of slavery and bring them to freedom. Passover reminds all Jews to honor their history and to praise God, who gave us new lives.

The story of Passover, Pesach in Hebrew, is found in the Book of Exodus, the second book of the Torah. More than three thousand years ago, the Israelites took refuge in Egypt, after a famine in their homeland. At first, the Israelites were welcome; their ancestor Joseph had been an important advisor to the pharaoh, or king, of Egypt. But as hundreds of years passed, and the Israelites grew in number, the Egyptians began to hate and fear them. Pharaoh decreed that the Israelites would become slaves, working out their days in the blazing Egyptian heat.

Then came an edict even worse than slavery. The Pharaoh ordered that every baby boy born to an Israelite be drowned in the Nile River. One baby, however, was saved from this horror. This child, who would be known as Moses, was placed by his mother, Jochebed, and his sister, Miriam, in a cradle of bulrushes and set afloat. He was found by Pharaoh's daughter, who raised him as her own son in the palace.

Yet Moses knew that he was an Israelite. As he grew older, he became angry at the way his people were treated. One day, he saw an Egyptian overseer beating an Israelite.

Moses struck and killed the overseer. Realizing his own life was in danger, he fled to the land of Midian.

Moses spent many years there. He married a woman named Zipporah, and tended the flocks of sheep owned by her father, Jethro. Life did not change much from one day to the next. Then a miracle occurred. While his sheep grazed, Moses saw a thorn bush burst into flame. Amazingly, the bush was not consumed. From the bush came the voice of God, who commanded Moses to go to Egypt and set the children of Israel free.

At first, Moses was afraid, because he thought he was not a leader. He found speaking difficult. But finally, with his brother Aaron, he made the journey back to Egypt. There he stood before Pharaoh and said, "Let my people go."

The Pharaoh saw no reason to do any such thing. So God sent ten plagues to the Egyptian people. There was a plague of blood in the Nile River; plagues of skin and cattle disease; wild beasts, frogs, lice, and locusts; plagues of darkness and hail.

But the will of Pharaoh was broken only by the terrible tenth plague: the firstborn male child in every Egyptian home was slain by the Angel of Death. Israelite families were spared. God had commanded them to dab the doorposts of their homes with the blood of a lamb as a sign for the Angel of Death to pass over the Jewish houses. This is where the name Passover comes from.

After the tenth plague, Pharaoh told the Israelites to leave Egypt. Rushing to gather their things, they baked bread that didn't have time to leaven, or rise. Similar crackers are today called *matzoh*, and they are an important symbol of Passover.

The Israelites fled Egypt, but almost as soon they were gone, Pharaoh decided that he wanted his slaves back.

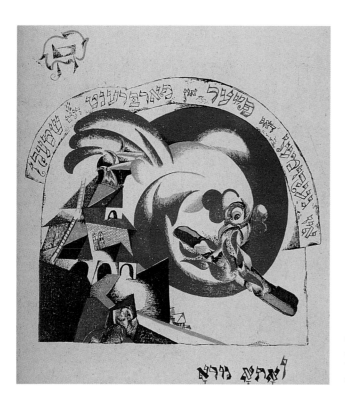

El Lissitzky, *Had Gadya Suite (Tale of a Goat)*, "Then Came a Fire and Burnt the Stick," 1919. The seder ends with the song "Had Gadya." In this illustration of the song by the artist El Lissitzky, a fire has come along to burn the stick that hit the dog that bit the cat that ate the goat. What comes next to put out the fire?

He sent his army in chariots to follow them, and they caught up with the Israelites on the banks of the Red Sea. The terrified Israelites despaired. The sea was ahead of them, the Egyptian army behind. But Moses prayed to God, and the Lord parted the Red Sea so the Israelites could cross.

When Pharaoh's army tried to follow, the waters closed upon them and swallowed them up. At last the Israelites were free! Moses' sister, Miriam, led the people in rejoicing with song and timbrels (an instrument similar to a tambourine). Their hope was to reach Canaan, the Promised Land beyond the River Jordan. It was a journey that was to take forty long years.

No holiday unites the Jews more than Passover. On the fifteenth of Nissan, Jews all over the world celebrate the festival of freedom. Passover is an eight-day holiday in which the Jewish community, family by family, recalls an important part of its history and gives expression to its hopes for the future.

But before Passover begins, there is much preparation and work that needs to be done. Since it comes in the spring, Passover is a holiday of freshness and new beginnings as well as freedom and rebirth. Part of getting ready for Passover is cleaning out and cleaning up. Most important, there must be no *chametz* in the house. Chametz is any food that has leavened or risen, or to which yeast has been added. That means bread, cakes, cookies, and many more of the things we eat every day. Anything that touches any of these sorts of food is also considered chametz.

All chametz should be disposed of or given away before Passover. In many homes, each crumb of chametz is searched out—in drawers, closets, even pockets—and thrown away. All this is done to remind people that the Israelites left Egypt in such haste that they could bring only unleavened bread with them.

Once the chametz is removed, the rest of the house is scrubbed and cleaned as well—a shiny start to a new season. This is also a good time to give away old toys and clothes to others who can use them.

Passover begins soon after sundown with a home service called a seder. Many families also host a seder the next night. The seder (which means order in Hebrew) incorporates a dinner with good food shared

by family and friends, but more important, the seder is a cere-mony and a lively exchange of ideas, in which those at the table, from oldest to youngest, talk about the meaning of Passover—and truly embrace that meaning.

The Passover table, always beautifully set, has several important elements. A pillow rests on the chair of the person who will lead the seder. The pillow is a symbol of relaxation. A free person has the right to rest or recline, a choice that is not available to a slave.

In front of the leader's place is a large plate that holds the five symbols of Passover. There is the *maror*, or bitter herbs; often horserad-ish is used. The maror is eaten to remind Jews of their bitter bondage in Egypt. *Haroset* is a mixture of apples, nuts, and wine. This sticky substance looks like the mortar the Israelites used to build the structures of Egypt, while its sweetness represents the hope of a better world.

Also on the plate is the *zeroah*, the shank bone of a lamb, as a reminder of the lamb's blood that was dabbed on the doorways. The *beitzah*, a roasted egg, is a symbol of life. Finally, there is *karpas*, fresh greens, most often parsley or lettuce. A symbol of spring, the karpas also brings to mind the new life of the Jews after they were freed from slavery. On the seder table is a small dish of salt water in which the karpas will be dipped. Salty, like the Red Sea, it is also makes us think of the tears shed by the Israelites.

Another plate on the Passover table holds three pieces of matzot, two for blessing, and one to be broken by the leader during the seder. One of the broken pieces is placed in a napkin or cloth envelope, and, during the eve-ing, an adult hides it. This special piece of matzot is called the *afikomen*, and the children at the seder are expected to find it. Whoever finds the afikomen can redeem it for a small gift, because the afikomen is needed at the end of the seder.

At every place on the Passover table is a small book, the Haggadah,

James Jacques Joseph Tissot, *Pharaoh's Daughter Receives the Mother of Moses*. Artist James Tissot painted many Bible stories, including this picture of baby Moses with Pharaoh's daughter and his mother.

which is read throughout the service. It contains prayers, and songs, and readings from the Bible. There are many versions of the Haggadah; some are as simple as a stapled booklet, others are gloriously illustrated.

Different families conduct their seders in different ways, but a seder usually takes several pleasant hours to complete. As with every Sabbath or holiday dinner, the meal begins with the blessing over the candles and the blessing over the wine. The first of four glasses of wine is sipped. Using a pitcher of water, a bowl, and a cloth, the leader washes his or her hands. Then the greens are dipped in the salt water and are passed around for everyone to taste. After the middle piece of matzoh is split and set aside as the afikomen, it is time for the telling of the story to begin.

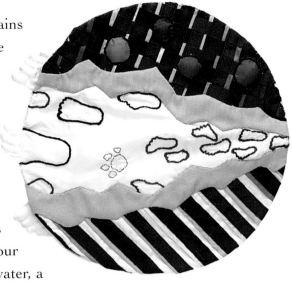

Jet Naftaniel-Joels, *"Steps" Matzoh Bag*, The Netherlands, 1993. This bag holds the three matzohs used at the seder. The footprints also remind us of the long journey of the ancient Jews from Egypt to the Promised Land.

The retelling of the Passover story begins with the words, "Why is this night different from all other nights?" The youngest child at the table then asks the Four Questions: "Why on this night do we eat unleavened bread?" "Why do eat bitter herbs?" "Why do we dip in the salt water?" "Why do we recline?"

The Haggadah addresses the four questions by telling the story of the Jews in Egypt and how they escaped to freedom. As the leader reads about the ten plagues, everyone dips his or her little finger in the glass of wine that is before them. A drop of wine is spilled on each person's plate for each plague. This act, "the lessening of our joy," reminds us that the Egyptians were also children of God, and we remember their suffering with sadness. Biblical quotations and rabbinic commentaries as well as folktales are all a part of the seder and are meant to provoke discussion.

More blessings follow. During this time the afikomen "disappears." The matzoh is blessed and eaten. The maror, the bitter herbs, are eaten with the haroset, the sweet apple mixture. Then the maror is eaten with matzoh. Now it is time for the dinner to begin.

The seder dinner is a very special one, and all sorts of special food are served. Every family has its own traditions, and everyone has a favorite seder dish. Sometimes matzoh ball soup starts the meal. Chicken or fish or turkey is often the main course. Side dishes might include *tzimmes,* a sweet stew of fruits and vegetables, or gefilte fish, ground fish

Arnold Eagle, *Passover Seder: Ritual Handwashing*, 1940s. An American family celebrates Passover in the 1940s. Does this look like your family's seder?

boiled with onions, carrots, and spices. Special casseroles called kugels, spicy or sweet, are made with matzoh rather than noodles, as at other times of the year.

Sephardic Jews, those whose ancestors come from the Middle East, enjoy different traditional dishes, such as caponata, a spicy eggplant stew, and pastelicos, fried mashed potato balls filled with meat.

The seder meal ends with the finding of the afikomen by the children. Without the afikomen, the seder cannot proceed, so the children ransom it back to the leader for a small gift or a coin.

However, there is still one guest who has not arrived. After the afikomen has been found, and the grace after the meal has been said, the seder guests open the front door, and the family invites the prophet Elijah to enter. It is said that Elijah, who gives aid and comfort to the poor, will announce the coming of the Messiah. Elijah brings with him the promise of a better world, one in which there is no more hunger, poverty, or war. A goblet of wine awaits him. The door is open—is that just a sudden breeze, or is it Elijah himself? Watch the wine glass—does it hold just a little bit less?

"Next year in Jerusalem." These words, the last of the seder, had special meaning to us when the Jews were without a homeland. Now that we are able to visit Jerusalem, "Next year in Jerusalem" represents the hope that soon all people will be free. Perhaps this will be the year that we are all united in a world of peace and love, at home and around the world.

Passover Activities

Haroset

This important part of the Passover seder is easy to make and tastes great on the seder plate or off. Ask an adult for help chopping the apples.

Ingredients:

1/2 pound walnuts, chopped

4 large Granny Smith apples, peeled and chopped
  into small pieces

1/2 cup red grape juice

1/4 pound dried pitted prunes, chopped (optional)

1. Combine nuts, apples, and prunes if desired.

2. Add grape juice.

3. Blend until mixture sticks together.

4. Refrigerate.

5. Enjoy during the seder and all through Passover.

Ludwig Y. Wolpert, *Passover Set*, Frankfurt, Germany, 1930. Wolpert used round shapes for the three matzoh trays, six food containers, and cup of Elijah on his Passover set. Try to imagine what it would look like if he had used triangles, rectangles, or squares.

Nodar Djindjihashvili, *Baking of Matzot, Tbilisi,* c.1980. Whether the matzoh is made in New York City or in Tbilisi, in the Republic of Georgia, the recipe for making the unleavened bread is always the same—flour, water, and nothing else.

Afikomen Cover

The afikomen, the special piece of matzoh hidden during the seder, needs a special covering. This cover can be used year after year.

Materials:
1 large white cloth napkin, pressed
needle and thread (use with adult help)
markers
scraps of material
glue

1. Fold the napkin horizontally.

2. Sew the two sides of the napkin nearest the fold.

3. Decorate both sides of the napkin with symbols of the holiday: a matzoh, an egg, a picture of Moses and his sister, Miriam. Or use the scraps of material to cut out the letters of the word *afikomen* and carefully glue them to the napkin.

4. Give the afikomen cover to the seder leader before the seder. The afikomen will fit neatly into its cover and be protected during its adventures.

Yom Ha-Shoah

Today the world knows that six million Jews and other people died during the Holocaust. Yom Ha-Shoah, Holocaust Remembrance Day, is when we remember those who lost their lives to the senseless horror of Nazi tyranny. The Israeli government designated the twenty-seventh of Nissan for the commemoration, the anniversary of the 1943 Warsaw Ghetto uprising, in which men, women, and children fought the Nazis against incredible odds. Though the ghetto was destroyed, the heroism of these Jewish martyrs inspires us today.

Yom Ha-Shoah is a day that touches all of us very

Yevgeny Khaldei, *Liberation of the Jewish Ghetto*, 1945. During World War II, the Nazis forced Jews to wear Stars of David on their clothes. It was part of the Nazis' plan to make the Jews feel different and inferior.

deeply. There is no proscribed way to spend this day, but many people go to services in the synagogue, and they light candles to remember the dead. Other people spend the day reading about the Holocaust, books like Anne Frank's diary or the writings of Holocaust survivor Elie Wiesel. Sometimes Yom Ha-Shoah is different just because it makes us stop, and think, and remember, and mourn.

The Holocaust is a sad and difficult thing to think about. But only by remembering the horror of the past can we protect the future.

Lasar Segall, *Exodus I*, 1947. The Holocaust forced many millions of people to leave their homes and families. Lasar Segall's painting gives us a glimpse of this sorrowful time.

Sally Soames, *Untitled*, 1979. When the Nazis took people from their homes during the Holocaust, they told them they could take one bag with them to their new homes in the East. Most of these people were, in fact, sent to death camps. These suitcases, once filled with cherished possessions, serve as a stark memorial to those who died.

Yom Ha-Shoah Activities

Many fine books have been written about the Holocaust. The most famous is *The Diary of a Young Girl* by Anne Frank, the moving story of a Dutch girl who died in the Bergen-Belsen concentration camp after years of hiding in an attic in Amsterdam.

Here is a list of other Holocaust books that will enhance your understanding of that terrible time in Jewish history.

Behind the Bedroom Wall by Laura Williams.

Karinna is a member of the Hitler Youth. When she learns her parents are hiding Jews, she must decide what is important to her and where her loyalties truly lie.

Daniel's Story by Carol Matas.

Fourteen-year-old Daniel is transported from his life in Frankfurt, Germany, to the horror of concentration camps Auschwitz and Buchenwald, all the while recording the horrors he sees with a smuggled camera.

The Devil's Arithmetic by Jane Yolen.

Hannah is tired of hearing about the Holocaust. But when she opens the door for the prophet Elijah one Passover night, she goes back in time to Poland in the 1940s, where she observes the terror of Nazism firsthand.

Jacob's Rescue by Malka Drucker.

During one memorable Passover in Israel, eight-year-old Marissa hears the story of her father's and uncle's experiences as children in the Warsaw Ghetto.

Number the Stars by Lois Lowry.

In this Newbery Award–winning book, a Danish girl, ten-year-old Annemarie, must help her friend Ellen Rosen escape to Sweden as the Nazis begin their roundup of the Danish Jews.

Yom Ha'atzma'ut

ome Jewish holidays celebrate ancient miracles. Yom Ha'atzma'ut celebrates a modern miracle: the founding of the state of Israel. Israel Independence Day takes place on the fifth day of Iyar, which comes during late April or early May. The holiday commemorates Israel's victory in the War of Independence. This victory, against overwhelming odds, allowed Israel to declare itself a state on May 14, 1948.

But before the celebration begins, the fallen soldiers of Israel are remembered on the solemn day of Yom Ha-Zikaron, on the fourth of Iyar. In Israel, a siren sounds at eleven in the morning, bringing the country to a halt. Prayers are offered for those who have fought and died in Israel's wars, defending an independent homeland for the Jewish people. A memorial service with lit torches is held at the Israeli National Cemetery on Mount Herzl; people light memorial candles in their homes.

Michal Ronnen Safdie, *Cross Roads*, from *The Western Wall*, 1994–95. Just beyond this ordinary courtyard in the old city of Jerusalem lies the Western Wall—the holiest place in the world for Jews. Why do you think the artist chose to take a picture of this spot?

Marcel Janco, *Ma'aberoth in Gray,* c. 1950. In the early days of the state of Israel, many new immigrants lived in ma'aberoth, or "tent cities," until housing was built for them. Looking at the colors and shapes in Marcel Janco's painting, what do you think conditions were like for these new immigrants?

At seven in the evening, a siren signals the end of Yom Ha-Zikaron, and immediately the mood in the country changes. The Israeli flag, which has flown at half mast, is proudly raised to full height. Dancing begins in the streets, and fireworks light up the sky. The holiday is also celebrated with picnics, parades, air shows, and other festivities.

Jews who do not live in Israel also want to celebrate the establishment of the Jewish homeland. In the United States, there are wonderful fairs and parties, with folk dancing, singing, and storytelling, plus tasty Israeli treats of every kind.

The ongoing strife in the Middle East has made the fifty-plus years of Israel's history tumultuous. Yet the very existence of Israel is a blessing for which Jews everywhere feel profoundly grateful. Whether we live in Israel or have been there or just hope to visit one day, we hold the Holy Land in our hearts.

Yom Ha'atzma'ut Activities

Hummus

Celebrate Israel Independence day with a festive meal that include some traditional Israeli dishes such as falafel, tabouli, and hummus. Here is a recipe for hummus that is simple to make with adult help.

Ingredients:
1 cup canned chickpeas, drained (keep
   2 tablespoons of liquid)
2 cloves of fresh garlic
juice of a small lemon
1 cup tahini sesame paste, stirred
1 teaspoon olive oil
salt and pepper

1. With the help of an adult, use a food processor to finely mince the garlic.

2. Add to the food processor bowl the chickpeas, lemon juice, and tahini. Add olive oil slowly.

3. The hummus is done when the texture is right for spreading.

4. Serve hummus with pita bread or vegetables.

Israeli Flag

Israel's flag features the traditional star of David. Make this flag and wave it proudly!

Materials:
white shirt cardboard
blue tempera paint or marker
flat stick from a crafts store,
   about 12 inches long

1. Lay the cardboard flat.

2. About 1 inch from the bottom long edge of the cardboard, paint or color a blue strip along the length of the board. Do the same at the top.

3. In the center of the cardboard, draw a blue star of David.

4. After the flag is dry, staple it to stick.

5. Wave!

Louis Goldman, *Israel Independence Day, Tel Aviv, May 1949*. The city of Tel Aviv becomes a teeming sea of people, as men, women, and children celebrate the first anniversary of Israel's founding. Israel turned one in 1949. How old is it today?

Shavuot

Like so many other Jewish holidays, Shavuot has two meanings. It is both a harvest celebration, a commemoration of the ripening of the first fruits of the spring harvest, and a celebration of another of God's gifts to us: the Ten Commandments.

The word *shavuot* means "weeks" in Hebrew, and Shavuot comes seven weeks after Passover. Shavuot celebrates the harvesting of wheat in Israel and the ripening of the first fruits. In ancient days, when the Temple, the house of God built by King Solomon, was in Jerusalem, farmers brought fruits and grains from their first spring harvest—dates, pomegranates, grapes, olives, wheat, and figs—as an offering of thanks. Shavuot is sometimes called the "Holiday of First Fruits."

Shavuot is also called the "Season of the Giving of the Law" because tradition says this is the time when Moses received the Ten Commandments from God on Mount Sinai. The Ten Commandments are the foundation for the Jewish religion, and for the moral law of countries throughout the world. The Ten Commandments tell people they must not worship false gods or take the name of the Lord in vain. It forbids murder, theft, adultery, envy, bearing false witness. It tells people they must honor their parents and remember the Sabbath and keep it holy.

Today Shavuot is celebrated for two days except in Israel, where it is a one-day holiday. At home, two candles are lit, symbolizing the two tablets of the Ten Commandments.

Abraham Schulkin, *Torah Ark from Adath Jeshurun Synagogue*, Sioux City, Iowa, 1899. A beautiful Torah ark (left) honors the Torah on Shavuot and throughout the year. This ark was carved by an Eastern European immigrant to the United States. Where did Schulkin get his ideas? Look at this wall hanging (right, Israel Dov Rosenbaum, *Decoration for the Eastern Wall [Mizrah]*, Podkamien, Ukraine, 1877.) It was created in the Ukraine, in the traditional Eastern European style. Abraham Schulkin was probably very familiar with Torah arks like the one Rosenbaum showed.

Challahs may be baked in two loaves that are joined together, also in commemoration of the tablets. Many Shavuot meals feature dairy products and fruit and vegetables rather than meat, to honor the harvest.

Some people stay up all night on Shavuot, studying Torah. Perhaps it was a scholar who started the belief that on midnight of the first night of the holiday, the heavens open. If you make a wish right then, it will be granted. Is it true? Why not try?

At the synagogue, which is decorated with flowers and greens, the Book of Ruth is read. This story of faith and devotion takes place during the harvest season. Ruth, a convert who has lost her husband, refuses to abandon her mother-in-law, Naomi, when Naomi decides to return to Judea. The women arrive at the time of the barley festival, and Ruth begins working in the fields of a wealthy landowner. Later she remarries, and from Ruth, a convert to Judaism, comes a new family. The Book of Ruth tells us a story of rebirth and renewal. Ruth's children went on to have many children of their own, and one of her descendants was

King David, who, tradition tells us, was born and later died on Shavuot.

A Shavuot custom in many synagogues is the confirmation ceremony in which teenage boys and girls are welcomed into the community of the congregation. Confirmation ceremonies are held during this holiday because the Torah was received on Shavuot, and this is the time the Israelites were initiated into the freedom and responsibility of their new religion.

Younger children just starting Hebrew school may also be brought to the temple for a special celebration of learning. In ancient times, young scholars first starting to read Hebrew were rewarded with a dab of honey so that their first taste of Torah would be sweet, and today the rabbi may give children a piece of honey candy as they start their journey.

Shavuot is a holiday of sweetness, as we rejoice in God's many gifts. Whether these gifts are as down-to-earth as an apple or as spiritual as the Commandments, they are the signs of God's love for all people.

Moritz Daniel Oppenheim, *Shavuot (Pentecost)*, 1880. The artist has used symbols of Shavuot to capture the essence of the holiday. The most important symbol is the Torah itself. What other symbols do you see?

Shavuot Activities

Fruit Compote

This simple recipe contains different varieties of fruit and is easy to serve at a family meal. It is especially tasty over blintzes.

Ingredients:
16-ounce can peaches, drained
16-ounce can pears, drained
8-ounce package dried apricots
16-ounce can cherry pie filling
juice of one lemon
juice of one orange
1/2 cup raisins

1. Cut peaches, pears, and apricots into bite-size pieces

   (ask an adult for help when using a knife). Put fruit into a large mixing bowl.

2. Add the cherry pie filling. Mix well.

3. Add the citrus juices to the mixture. Stir well.

4. Sprinkle in the raisins and stir once more.

5. Warm, either in the oven or the microwave (be sure compote is in a safe container for heating).

6. Serve warm or at room temperature.

Fruit Centerpiece

Use this centerpiece for your holiday table, and then let your guests take pieces of the fruit as a part of the dessert.

Materials:

Styrofoam cone or ball

aluminum foil

pieces of fruit cut up

    with adult assistance, enough to cover the

    Styrofoam mold: grapes, cantaloupe, pineapple,

    strawberries, pitted cherries.

wooden toothpicks

lettuce

decorative dish

1. Cover Styrofoam with aluminum foil.

2. Starting at the bottom and working toward the top, cover the mold with fruit. Use a toothpick to pierce each piece of fruit, keeping the piece as close to one end of the toothpick as possible. Insert the other end of the toothpick into the Styrofoam so the fruit lies up against the mold.

3. Working in a circular fashion, add more pieces of fruit. Pack the fruit together as tightly as you can so that no foil shows.

4. Place lettuce leaves on the plate, and put fruit centerpiece on the lettuce.

Simcha, wife of Menahem Levi Meshullami, *Torah Ark Curtain* (detail), Venice, 1680–81. On this Torah ark covering, a mountain hovers over the city of Jerusalem as the hands of God extend a set of tablets almost as big as the mountain itself.

Tisha B'Av

How many sad things can happen on the same day? In Jewish history, several tragic events have occurred on the ninth day of Av, which comes during the summer.

Two of those events concern the Temple in Jerusalem, the heart of Jewish worship in ancient days. King Solomon built the first temple, a magnificent building described in the Bible as made of the finest wood and decorated with gold. But it is not remembered simply for its beauty. The Temple was where all the ceremonies of Jewish life took place. It was where the Jewish people brought their offerings, especially on Sukkot, Passover, and Shavuot.

On the ninth day of Av in 586 B.C.E., Solomon's Temple was destroyed by the Babylonian army of King Nebuchadnezzar. Using chariots and battering rams, the well-equipped army conquered the country, setting fire to Jerusalem and looting the Temple.

The Jews were permitted to return to their homeland seventy years later, and the Temple was

Shalom of Safed, *Levites Playing Music in the Holy Temple,* 1972. Rows of musicians play at this version of the Temple.

rebuilt. For almost six hundred years, the second Temple remained in use (though at one time it was defiled and had to be restored by the Maccabees, as the Hanukkah story tells us).

In 70 C.E., the all-powerful Roman army, which had taken control of Judea, finally quelled a Jewish uprising that had begun several years earlier. On the ninth of Av, the Romans stormed into Jerusalem. They destroyed the city, including the Temple, and killed thousands, marching the rest into exile and slavery. All that remains of the Temple is its Western Wall, a site of pilgrimage and prayer today.

Tradition says another tragedy took place on the ninth of Av. Simon Bar Kochba and his band of rebels made their last stand at the mountain fortress of Betar, where they were finally defeated and killed on that day in 135 B.C.E.

Moses Formstecher, *Bottle Containing Model of Jeruselem Temple*, Offenbach, Germany, 1813. No one is sure what the Temple really looked like. This artist has created one version. How do you think he got it into the bottle?

Centuries later in Spain, the Catholic church and the King Philip and Queen Isabella of Spain decided to rid themselves of the Jews who had long lived in their country. The Church instituted the Inquisition, in part to convert Jews to Christianity. Through intimidation and torture, many did convert, but some people continued to practice Judaism in secret. They were called Marranos, and if discovered, their lives were in jeopardy.

In 1492, the same year that Columbus arrived in America, the king and queen of Spain ordered all the Jews of Spain to convert or leave the country. On the ninth day of Av, by sea and over land, thousands of Jews departed the country that had been their home for so many years.

On Tisha B'Av, a book of the Bible called Lamentations is read during the synagogue service. This sad book describes the sorrow of the prophet Jeremiah, who watched Jerusalem being ravaged by the Babylonians. Some Jews observe the day as a fast day and a mourning period, and in synagogues the ark that houses the Torah scrolls is draped in black. In Israel, people pray at the Western Wall in Jerusalem, all that remains of the second Temple destroyed by the Romans so long ago. And while we mourn the loss of the Temples, and our exile from Israel for so many, many years, today we also rejoice at being able to pray in Jerusalem once again.

Tisha B'Av Activities

Tisha B'Av Kaleidoscope

Destruction and rebuilding are part of the story of Judaism. Sometimes the rebuilding is real, like the establishment of Israel so many years after the destruction of the Temple. Sometimes it is metaphorical, like the way we reexamine our lives during the High Holy Days and try to build a better world for ourselves and those around us.

If you have ever looked through a kaleidoscope, you know that from broken bits and pieces come beauty and order. Make this simple kaleidoscope, and in it you will see a unified whole that, like Judaism itself, is more than the sum of its parts.

Materials:

duct tape

three pieces of acrylic mirror or mirror board, all
    equal rectangles 3 inches wide and 8 inches long

shirt cardboard

paper punches in different shapes

tracing paper

clear acetate

tiny beads, sequins, small plastic jewels, or scraps
    of colorful thin paper (such as origami paper)

tracing paper

1. Using the duct tape, tape the mirrors together (shiny side in) to make a long triangular "tube."

2. Cut a piece of shirt cardboard into a triangle the same size as the end of your mirror tube. Use a round paper punch to make a small, round hole in the middle. Tape the cardboard across one end of the mirror tube.

3. Cut a triangle of tracing paper and one of clear acetate.

4. Tape the two pieces together on two sides to form a pocket.

5. Put a few beads, sequins, jewels, or paper scraps (cut with the paper punches) into the pocket.

6. Tape the pocket shut, and tape it to the open end of the mirror tube.

7. Hold the kaleidoscope up to the light and look through the peephole. Turn as you look. You can make extra pockets for your kaleidoscope. Change them as often as you like, to see more beautiful patterns.

Photography Credits

All photographs are courtesy of The Jewish Museum, New York, and copyright © The Jewish Museum, New York. Photos on the following pages are by John Parnell: 9, 17, 29, 30, 43, 44, 45, 46, 49, 51, 54, 56, 59, 61, 62, 63, 64 (top), 69, 71. Page numbers are given in bold.

Frontispiece Marc Chagall (Russian, 1887–1985), *The Story of Exodus: Moses Receives the Ten Commandments*, 1966. Color lithograph, 18⅜ x 13 in. (46.7 x 34.3 cm). Gift of Herman and Sietske Turndorf, 1982-231.14. © 2002 Artists Rights Society (ARS), New York / ADAGP, Paris. Photo: Richard Goodbody.
7 *Sabbath Cloth*, Persia, 1806. Cotton: embroidered with polychrome silk, diameter 32⅝ in. (83 cm). Gift of Dr. Harry G. Friedman, F 4007. Photo: Joseph Sachs.
8 *Torah Crown*, Galicia, 1764/65; 1773 (inscriptions). Silver: cast, repousse, cut-out, engraved, parcel-gilt; semi-precious stones, glass stones, 19¼ x diam. 8⅝ in. (49 x 22 cm). Gift of Dr. Harry G. Friedman, F 2585.
9 Isidor Kaufmann (Austrian, 1853–1921), *Friday Evening*, c. 1920. Oil on canvas, 28½ x 35½ in. (72.4 x 90.2 cm). Gift of Mr. and Mrs. M. R. Schweitzer, JM 4-63.
11 *Havdalah Set: Plate, Kiddush Cup, Spice Container, and Candlestick.* Jerusalem, 1950-55. Maker: Ludwig Y. Wolpert (American, b. Germany, 1900–1981). Silver: cut-out. Plate: diam. 8⅛ in. (20.6 cm). Kiddush cup: 5½ in. (14 cm). Spice container: 5½ in. (14 cm). Candlestick: 3 in. (7.6 cm). Gift of the Abram and Frances Kanof Collection, JM 39-60 a-d.
15 *Jewish New Year's Greeting*, Nome, Alaska, 1910. Attributed to Happy Jack (Inuit, c. 1870–1918). Engraved walrus tusk with gold inset, 10 x 1 in. (25.4 x 2.5 cm). Gift of Kanofsky Family in memory of Minnie Kanofsky, 1984-71. Photo: Coxe-Goldberg Photography.
16 Gabriel Cohen (Israeli, b. 1933), *The Creation of the World*, 1980. Acrylic on canvas, 25½ x 37½ in. (64.8 x 95.8 cm). Museum purchase with funds donated by Greta M. Koppel in memory of her beloved husband, Rudolph F. Koppel, 1981-232. Photo: John Back.
17 Chester Higgins, Jr. (American, b. 1946), *Commandment Keepers Congregation Harlem (High Holidays)*, 1989. Gelatin-silver print, 16 x 20 in. (40.6 x 50.8 cm). Museum purchase, Gift of Mr. and Mrs. Kurt Olden, by exchange 1995-31.
18 *New Year's Greeting Card–Family Meal.* Germany or United States, early 1900s. Embossed paper: printed and cut-out, 9 1/16 x 9 x 5⅛ in. (23.2 x 22.9 x 13 cm). Gift of Mildred and George Weissman, 1999-9. Photo: Richard Goodbody
21 Ben Shahn (American, b. Lithuania, 1898–1969). *Today Is the Birthday of the World*, 1955. Ink on paper, 22 ½ x 31 in. (57.2 x 78.7 cm). Gift of Mr. and Mrs. Albert A. List Family, JM 88-72. © Estate of Ben Shahn / Licensed by VAGA, New York.
22 *Belt Buckle for the High Holidays*, Poland, 1863. Silver, 4 ¾ x 2 ½ in. (12.1 x 6.4 cm). Gift of Dr. Harry G. Friedman, F 3194.
24 Harriete Estel Berman (American, b. 1952), *Tzedakah* (alms container), 1999. Pre-printed steel, aluminum rivets, 55 x 35 in. (139.7 x 88.9 cm). Museum purchase with funds given by the Dr. Joel and Phyllis Gitlin Judaica Acquisitions Fund, 2001-8a-xx.
26 *Alms Container*, Denmark, 1901. Pewter: cast, 4⅞ x 2¾ x 3⅞ in. (12.4 x 7.0 x 9.8 cm). Purchased with funds given by the Helen and Jack Cytryn Fund, 2000-52.
28 *Sukkah Decoration*, Trieste, Italy, c. 1775. Maker: Israel David Luzzatto. Ink and watercolor on paper. 20 x 15½ in. (50.8 x 39.4 cm). The H. Ephraim and Mordecai Benguiat Family Collection, S 256.
29 Leopold Pilichowski (Polish, 1869-1933), *Sukkoth*, 1894–95. Oil on canvas, 42½ x 53 in. (108 x 134.6 cm). Gift of Mr. and Mrs. Oscar Gruss, JM 89-55. This painting may have been in the collection of Isser and Friedl Reifer, Vienna.
30 Louis Goldman (American, b. Germany, 1925–1996). *Sukkoth Market, Tel Aviv, September 1953.* Black and white fiber-based print, 11 x 14 in. (27.9 x 35.6 cm). Museum purchase with funds provided by Gaby and Curtis Hereld 1994-716.
33 *Simchat Torah Flag*, Poland, 1800s. Woodcut on paper, 6 3/16 x 7½ in. (16.2 x 19.1 cm). The Rose and Benjamin Mintz Collection, M 605.
34 *Torah Shield*, Nuremberg, c. 1720. Silver: cast, engraved, parcel-gilt, 10½ x 12 in. (26.6 x 30.5 cm). Gift of Dr. Harry G. Friedman, F 3686.
35 Solomon Alexander Hart (British, 1806–1881), *The Feast of the Rejoicing of the Law at the Synagogue in Leghorn, Italy*, 1850. Oil on canvas, 55⅝ x 68¾ in. (141.3 x 174.6 cm). Gift of Mr. and Mrs. Oscar Gruss, JM 28-55. Photo: Nicholas Sapieha.
36 Larry Rivers (American, b. 1925), *Study for Maccabees II*, 1982. Pastel and colored pencil, 16 x 18¾ in. (40.6 x 47.6 cm). Gift of Sivia and Jeffrey H. Loria, 1983-301. © Larry Rivers / Licensed by VAGA, New York.
38 *Hanukkah Lamp, "Miss Liberty,"* Princeton, New Jersey, 1974. Maker: Mae Rockland Tupa (American, b. 1937). Wood covered in fabric with molded plastic figures, 11 x 24 x 7 in. (27.9 x 60.9 x 17.8 cm). Gift of the artist, 1984-127 a,b. Photo: Coxe-Goldberg Photography. *Hanukkah Lamp.* Maker: F. J. Kormis. London, England, 1950. Copper alloy, 16 x 13⅛ x 3 15/16 in. (40.6 x 33.3 x 10cm). Gift of Karl Nathan, JM 22-50.
39 *Hanukkah Lamp*, North Africa, c. 1900. Copper alloy, h. 12¾ in. (32.4 cm). Gift of Dr. Harry G. Friedman, F 3400.
40 *Hanukkah Lamp*, Stolin, Russia, c. 1885. Lead, 2⅜ x 1 x 1 in. (6 x 2.5 x 2.5 cm). Gift of the Chernick Family, JM 102-73. *Dreidels*, Poland, 1700s. Wood: carved, h. 2⅛ x 1 in. (5.4 x 2.5 cm). From the Rose and Benjamin Mintz Collection, M 301, M 302, M 305, M 306. Photo: Geoffery Clements.
43 *Executive Dreidel*, Artists: Bonnie Srolovitz and Michael Berkowicz, New York, 1993. Brass and silver. Purchased with funds given by the Judaica Acquisitions Fund, 1993-248.
44 Anna Ticho (Israeli, b. Austria, 1894–1980), *Jerusalem Hills*, 1978. Charcoal and pastel on paper, 33⅜ x 42½ in. (84.8. x 108 cm). Gift of Ellen and Jerome L. Stern, 1999-123.
45 Samuel Halpert (American, b. Russia, 1884–1930), *Trees*, 1917. Oil on canvas, 23 x 27 in. (58.4 x 68.6 cm). Gift of Dr. and Mrs. Wesley Halpert with donors maintaining life estate, 1990-145.
46 Annie Leibovitz (American, b. 1949), *Kibbutz Amir, Israel*, 1969. Gelatin-silver print, 16 x 20 in. (40.6 x 50.8 cm). Gift of the artist, 1994-59.
49 Mimi Gross (American, b. 1940), *Purim Mask: Wicked Haman, Queen Esther, King Ahasuerus*, 1964. Papier-maché, 28½ x 25 x 25 in. (72.4 x 63.5 x 63.5 cm). Gift of Chaim and Renee Gross, 1987-108.
50 Robert Indiana (American, b. 1928), *Purim: The Four Faces of Esther*, 1967. Silkscreen, 29 x 22½ in. (73.7 x 57.2 cm). Gift of Florence and Ralph Spencer, JM 109-67. © 2002 Morgan Art Foundation Ltd. / Artists Rights Society (ARS), New York.
52 *Esther Scroll*, Moravia (?), 1700s. Ink and gouache on parchment, h. 5 in. (12.7 cm). Gift of Dr. Harry G. Friedman, F 2130. *Purim Noisemaker*, New York, 1988. Maker: Moshe Zabari (Israeli, b. 1935). Silver: fabricated, cut-out; lapis lazuli: granulated; carnelian, 13½ x 6 3/16 in. (34.3 x 15.8 cm). Gift of the artist, 1988-31.
54 *Purim Noisemaker*, Russia, 1800s. Silver: cast, engraved, 20½ in. (52.1 cm). Benjamin and Rose Mintz Collection, M 295.
56 El Lissitzky (Russian, 1890–1941). *Had Gadya Suite (Tale of a Goat), "Then Came a Fire and Burnt the Stick,"* 1919. Colored lithograph on paper, 10¾ x 10 in. (27.3 x 25.4 cm). Gift of Leonard and Phyllis Greenberg, 1986-121g. © 2002 Artists Rights Society (ARS), New York / VG Bild-Kunst, Bonn.
58 James Jacques Joseph Tissot (French, 1836–1902), *Pharaoh's Daughter Receives the Mother of Moses.* Gouache, 8⅝ x 10 7/16 in. (22.5 x 26.5 cm). Gift of the heirs of Jacob H. Schiff, 1952-146.
59 *"Steps" Matzoh Bag*, The Netherlands, 1993. Maker: Jet Naftaniel-Joels (Dutch, b. 1950). Synthetic fabric on muslin lining: embroidered, and appliqué, diam. 12½ in. (31.8 cm). Gift of The Jewish Historical Museum, Amsterdam, 1993-154.
60 Arnold Eagle (American, 1909–1992), *Passover Seder: Ritual Handwashing*, 1940s. Gelatin-silver print, 7½ x 9½ in. (19.1 x 24.1 cm). Gift of Dorothy Eagle in memory of Arnold Eagle, 1993-106.
61 *Passover Set.* Frankfurt, Germany, 1930. Maker: Ludwig Y. Wolpert (American, b. Germany, 1900–1981). Silver, ebony and glass, 10 x 16 in. (25.4 x 40.6 cm). Promised gift of Sylvia Zenia Wiener.
62 Nodar Djindjihashvili (American, b. Russia 1939), *Baking of Matzot, Tbilisi*, c. 1978/80. Chromogenic color print, 12⅜ x 18 in. (31.5 x 45.7 cm). Museum purchase through funds provided by Stephen and Barbara Friedman, 1989-81.
63 Yevgeny Khaldei (Russian, 1917–1997), *Liberation of the Jewish Ghetto*, Budapest, January 1945. Gelatin-silver print. Gift of Howard Schickler, 1997-30.
64 Lasar Segall (Brazilian, b. Lithuania, 1881–1957), *Exodus I*, 1947. Oil on canvas, 54 x 52 in. (132 x 137.1 cm). Gift of James Rosenberg and George Baker in memory of Felix M. Warburg, JM 25-48. Sally Soames [b. Great Britain], *Untitled*, 1979. Gelatin-silver print. Gift of the artist, 1982-237.3. © Sally Soames.
66 Michal Ronnen Safdie (Israeli, b. 1951), *Cross Roads*, from *The Western Wall*, 1994–95. C-print. Gift of the artist in honor of Sara and Axel Schupf, 2001-7.3. Photo: Richard Goodbody.
67 Marcel Janco (Israeli, b. Romania, 1895–1984), *Ma'aberoth in Gray*, c. 1950. Oil on canvas, 30¾ x 38½ in. (78.1 x 97.8 cm). Gift of Alan Stroock, JM 28-63.
69 Louis Goldman (American, b. Germany, 1925-1996), *Independence Day, Tel Aviv, May 1949*, 1958. Fiber-based print, 14 x 11 in. (35.6 x 27.9 cm). Museum purchase with funds provided by the Lucy and Henry Moses Fund, 1994-715.
71 *Torah Ark from Adath Jeshurun Synagogue*, Sioux City, Iowa, United States, 1899. Carved by Abraham Schulkin. Carved pine, stained with gold colored paint, 120 1/16 x 96 1/16 x 29 15/16 in. (305 x 244 x 76 cm). Gift of the Jewish Federation of Sioux City, Iowa, JM 48-56. Photo: Coxe-Goldberg Photography. *Decoration for the Eastern Wall (Mizrah).* Artist: Israel Dov Rosenbaum. Podkamien, Ukraine, 1877. Paint, ink, and pencil on cut-out paper, 36 x 24 in. (91.4 x 61 cm). Gift of Helen W. Finkel in memory of Israel Dov Rosenbaum, Bessie Rosenbaum Finkel, and Sidney Finkel, 1987–136.
72 Moritz Daniel Oppenheim (German, 1800–1882), *Shavuot (Pentecost)*, 1880. Oil on canvas, 28 x 24 in. (71.1 x 61.0 cm). Gift of The Oscar and Regina Gruss Charitable and Educational Foundation, 1999–85. Photo: Richard Hori.
74 *Torah Ark Curtain*, Venice, 1680–81. Maker: Simcha, wife of Menahem Levi Meshullami. Silk embroidered with silk and metallic threads, metallic fringe, 85 1/16 x 55⅛ in. (216 x 140 cm). Gift of Professor Neppi Modona, Florence, through Dr. Harry G. Friedman, F 2944.
75 Shalom of Safed (Israeli, 1887–1980), *Levites Playing Music in the Holy Temple*, 1972. Acrylic on canvas, 24 x 24 in., Gift of Louis Stein, JM 54-72.
76 *Bottle Containing Model of Jerusalem Temple*, Offenbach, Germany, 1813. Maker: Moses Formstecher. Half-post blown glass; wood; painted wood; metal, 11¼ x 5 x diam. 5 in. (28.6 x 12.7 x 12.7 cm). Gift of Mr. and Mrs. Louis C. Bial, JM 21-79a,b.

Bibliography and further Reading

* Adler, David A. *The Kids' Catalog of Jewish Holidays.* Philadelphia: Jewish Publication Society, 1996.

* Berger, Gilda. *Stories of the Jewish Holidays.* New York: Scholastic, 1998.

Brinn, Ruth. *The Shabbat Catalogue.* Hoboken, N.J.: KTAV Publishing, 1978.

* Cuyler, Margery. *Jewish Holidays.* New York: Henry Holt, 1978.

* Burns, Marilyn. *The Hanukkah Book.* New York: Four Winds, 1981.

* Cederbaum, Sophie. *A First Book of Jewish Holidays.* New York: Union of Hebrew Congregations, 1995.

Domnitch, Larry. *The Jewish Holidays.* Montvale, N.J.: Jason Aronson, 2000.

* Drucker, Malka. *Hanukkah. Eight Nights, Eight Lights.* New York: Holiday House, 1980.

* Drucker, Malka. *Sukkot: A Time to Rejoice.* New York: Holiday House, 1982.

* Fishman, Cathy Goldberg. *On Rosh Hashana and Yom Kippur.* New York: Atheneum, 1997.

Ganz, Yaffa. *Follow the Moon: A Journey Through the Jewish Year.* Jerusalem and New York: Feldheim Publishers, 1984.

Greenberg, Blu. *How to Run a Traditional Jewish Household.* New York: Simon and Schuster, 1983.

* Hoyt-Goldsmith, Diane. *Celebrating Hanukkah.* New York: Holiday House, 1996.

Klagsbrun, Francine. *Jewish Days: A Book of Jewish Life and Culture Around the Year.* New York: Farrar, Straus and Giroux, 1996.

* Musleah, Rahel. *Why on This Night? A Passover Haggadah for Family Celebration.* New York: Simon and Schuster, 2000.

Renberg, Dalia Hardof. *The Complete Family Guide to Jewish Holidays.* New York: Adama Books, 1985.

* Rush, Barbara, and Schwartz, Cherie Karo. *The Kids' Catalog of Passover: A Worldwide Celebration.* Philadelphia: Jewish Publication Society, 2000.

Rush, Barbara. *The Jewish Year: Celebrating the Holidays.* New York: Stewart, Tabori and Chang, 2000.

Strassfeld, Michael. *The Jewish Holidays: Guide and Commentary.* New York: Harper and Row, 1978.

* Yolen, Jane. *Milk and Honey: A Year of Jewish Holidays.* New York: Putnam, 1990.

* *Suitable for young readers*

Index